Intermediate World History B, 8
Learning Coach Guide

Part 2

About K12 Inc.

K12 Inc., a technology-based education company, is the nation's leading provider of proprietary curriculum and online education programs to students in grades K–12. K¹² provides its curriculum and academic services to online schools, traditional classrooms, blended school programs, and directly to families. K12 Inc. also operates the K¹² International Academy, an accredited, diploma-granting online private school serving students worldwide. K¹²'s mission is to provide any child the curriculum and tools to maximize success in life, regardless of geographic, financial, or demographic circumstances. K12 Inc. is accredited by CITA. More information can be found at www.K12.com.

978-1-60153-327-2

Printed by RR Donnelley/Digital, Kendallville, IN, USA, July 2015

Table of Contents

Learning Coach Guide
Lesson 1: The World Turned Upside Down: The American Revolution

England's revolution just marked the beginning. Educated people in farflung places gathered to discuss what they read and thought about what had happened in England. They argued heatedly about what John Locke had said about the purpose of government. The more they talked and thought, the more dissatisfied they grew with the status quo. In France, in the British colonies in North America, and in the Spanish colonies of Latin America, the time had come for change. A revolution is just that—a dramatic change. The world was about to witness a series of revolutions. How many would succeed? How difficult would they be?

Lesson Objectives

- Summarize the attitude of most colonists toward Britain in 1763 and the reasons for their attitude.
- Explain why Parliament imposed taxes after 1763 and why the colonists reacted as they did.
- Describe the events that led to war between Britain and the colonies.
- Identify Montesquieu, Locke, and Jefferson and their political ideas.
- Summarize the arguments Thomas Paine put forth in *Common Sense,* and their influence on colonial opinion regarding independence.
- Summarize the major ideas of the Declaration of Independence.
- Identify George Washington and his contributions to the revolution.
- Describe the disadvantages the American army faced and the importance of French aid in winning the war.
- Summarize the reasons for a Constitutional Convention in 1787 and its accomplishments.
- Identify the U.S. Constitution as the world's oldest functioning written constitution.
- Review historical events.

PREPARE

Approximate lesson time is 60 minutes.

Materials

For the Student

    📖 Making Sense of Common Sense

    📖 Reading Guide

    The Human Odyssey, Volume 2 edited by Klee, Cribb, and Holdren

    History Journal

For the Adult

    📖 Lesson Answer Key

Keywords and Pronunciation

Enlightenment : era in the eighteenth century when thinkers valued logic, reason, and scientific method

tyranny : abuse of power; according to John Locke, the actions of a ruler who "makes not the law, but his will, the rule"

TEACH
Activity 1: Declaring and Winning Independence (Offline)
Instructions

Activity 1. Declaring and Winning Independence (Offline)

This lesson is designed to be completed in **3** class sessions.

Day 1
Read

Your student will read the Part 3 Introduction and Chapter 1, from the beginning to "Declaring Independence," pages 349–361, and complete **Day 1** of the Reading Guide. When your student has finished, he should use the Lesson Answer Key to check the work, and then place the Reading Guide in his History Journal.

Making Sense of *Common Sense*

Your student will complete the Putting Words in Thomas Paine's Mouth sheet and fill out the Collision Course chart showing how the attitude of most American colonists toward Britain changed from 1763 to the time Thomas Paine published *Common Sense* in 1776.

Day 2
Read

Your student will read Chapter 1, from "Declaring Independence" to the end of the chapter, pages 361–367, and complete **Day 2** of the Reading Guide. When your student has finished, he should use the Lesson Answer Key to check his work, and then place the Reading Guide in his History Journal.

Declaring Independence and Acting Independently

After reading the assignment, your student will go online to create a chronological list of events showing how the colonists proclaimed their freedom from Great Britain, won independence, and set up a new form of government for the United States.

No King? Now What?

Next, your student will see how the former colonists drew on Montesquieu's arguments and other ideas from the Enlightenment to form their government. An online activity will focus on the separation of powers and the functions of the three main branches of government.

Day 3
Asking the Tough Questions!

Your student will concentrate on the achievements of one particular character from Chapter 1 of Part 3. (He may need to go online to do some research about the person he chooses.) Your student will show what he has learned by pretending to be a newspaper reporter and interviewing the person he selected.

ASSESS

Lesson Assessment: The World Turned Upside Down: The American Revolution, Part 1 (*Online*)

Students will complete an online assessment based on the lesson objectives. The assessment will be scored by the computer.

Lesson Assessment: The World Turned Upside Down: The American Revolution, Part 2 (*Offline*)

Students will complete this part of the Lesson Assessment offline. Print the test and have students complete it on their own. Use the answer key to score the test, and then enter the results online. The attached answer key is the most current and may not coincide with previously printed guides.

TEACH

Activity 2. Optional: The World Turned Upside Down: The American Revolution (*Online*)

Instructions

Your student may want to spend additional time with the Declaration of Independence. To learn more, he should visit the United States Constitution website [http://www.house.gov/Constitution/Constitution.html] and the National Constitution Center [http://www.constitutioncenter.org/].

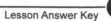

The World Turned Upside Down: The American Revolution

Day 1

Read

Reading Guide

1. The English philosopher who wrote, in his *Two Treatises of Government,* that all people have natural rights, was <u>John Locke</u>.

2. Name two rights that John Locke discussed.
    Life, liberty, and property

3. Why were Britain's colonists so proud to be part of the British Empire in 1763? Give at least two reasons.
    They had just helped defeat Britain's longtime rival, France, in the French and Indian War. They took pride in their English heritage because of their rights and freedoms as Englishmen.

4. Why did many colonists refer to Britain as "the mother country"?
    The great majority of North American colonists were of English descent.

5. True or false? Britain had always maintained careful control of the colonies, giving the appointed governors the power to tax and enact laws for the colonists.
    False

6. The colonists despised the new taxes imposed in 1765 by the <u>Stamp</u> Act. Why was it so named?
    This law said that most printed material—newspapers, pamphlets, almanacs, legal documents, even playing cards—could only be published on paper bearing an official stamp, which the colonists had to buy.

7. What did the colonists mean when they cried, "No taxation without representation"?
    They believed that governments had no right to raise money from the people without the consent of the people through their elected representatives.

8. Name the French Enlightenment author of *The Spirit of the Laws* who defined tyranny as "the exercise of power beyond right."
    Montesquieu

9. What was the Boston Massacre, and why did it upset people in the colonies so much?
    The Boston Massacre occurred in 1770 when British soldiers fired on a group of colonists who were protesting the presence of soldiers in their town. Five colonists died.

10. Why in 1773 did a group of colonists disguise themselves as Indians, make their way to Boston Harbor, and board three British cargo ships?
    The colonists resented the tax that Parliament had put on tea. To protest the tax, a group of disguised colonists split open the 342 crates of tea aboard the British cargo ships and tossed them into the harbor. Afterwards, colonists joked about the "Boston Tea Party."

11. What was "the shot heard 'round the world"?
    When British soldiers clashed with colonial militiamen in Lexington, Massachusetts, in 1775, the gunfire of the militiamen was, a poet later wrote, "the shot heard 'round the world."

12. What was *Common Sense* in the American Revolution?
    Common Sense was the name of a pamphlet published by Thomas Paine in 1776 that convinced many colonists to favor independence from Britain.

Putting Words in Thomas Paine's Mouth

1. Paine insisted that institutions of government should be reasonable. Was it reasonable for a king to rule colonies far away? Paine answered with a resounding <u>no</u>.

2. When Paine said, "Tis time to part," he meant that the colonies should become <u>independent</u> of Britain.

3. According to Paine, "Of more worth is one honest man to society" than a <u>king</u>.

4. Paine described a king as <u>someone whose ancestors had stolen other people's land at the point of a sword</u>.

5. To Paine, "there is something very absurd, in supposing a continent to be perpetually governed by an <u>island</u>."

6. Paine argued that "the parent of America" is not England but Europe. What evidence did he present for his argument?
    Answers may vary, but should include the idea that people had come from all parts of Europe to escape tyranny and seek civil and religious liberty in the colonies.

7. Paine argued that the king was not a proper power to govern the American people. Why?
    Paine argued that the king would have a negative effect on any government of this continent because he has shown himself to be an enemy of liberty.

Collision Course

British Point of View	Colonists' Point of View
Colonists should pay taxes to support the army.	Parliament cannot tax the colonists because the colonists are not represented in Parliament.
London should rule the colonies.	The colonies have successfully ruled themselves for 150 years.
A king should be head of the country.	Kings are tyrants. The colonists would be better off with no laws than with the king's laws.
The colonies should stay tied to "the mother country."	The colonies don't need a "mother country." It makes no sense for an island to rule a continent.

What was the result of these differing points of view?
    The colonies declared their independence.

Day 2

Read

Reading Guide

13. In the Declaration of Independence, Thomas Jefferson argued for certain "unalienable rights" that were endowed by the Creator. What were those rights?
    Answers may vary but should include: "life, liberty, and the pursuit of happiness"; the right to resist and replace a ruler who has become a tyrant; the right to abolish a government that is "destructive" of the people's freedoms

14. The leader of the Continental Army was George Washington. Name two of his achievements during the war.
    He showed great leadership. He kept his army together through the grueling winter at Valley Forge, ready to fight again. He promoted the Marquis de Lafayette to general in the army. He defeated the British at the battle of Yorktown.

15. What disadvantages did the Continental Army face?
    At the beginning of the war, the British had twice as many troops as the Continental Army. American soldiers often quarreled with each other and refused to take orders. The British army was well trained and disciplined. The British had a large number of German mercenaries.

16. Why did the Americans need French help?
    The French sent much-needed money, arms, and gunpowder to the Americans. The French had a powerful navy, which the Americans did not.

17. Colonists who remained loyal to Britain were known as Royalists or Tories.

18. The last major battle of the American Revolution was fought at Yorktown in Virginia.

19. The government for the new United States was described in a document called the Articles of Confederation. What weaknesses did this government have?
    Congress had very little power. It could not collect taxes. It could pass laws, but the states didn't have to obey them unless they wanted to. The Congress had no power to force states to meet their obligations. Each state passed its own regulations about commerce with foreign countries. States ignored treaties that didn't suit them. They decided whether or not to fight the Indians on the frontier. They built their own navies. States even printed their own money. The central government was weak and defenseless against its enemies.

20. Why did Americans call a Constitutional Convention in 1787?
    Answers may vary. They called a convention to draw up a constitution and to create a stronger central government. They wanted the thirteen states to behave more like a single nation. They needed to draw up common laws and regulations and protect themselves from foreign enemies. They were putting into effect the ideas of the Enlightenment.

21. What is unique about the U.S. Constitution?
    Answers may vary. It is the world's oldest functioning written constitution. It puts into effect the ideas of the Enlightenment. It guarantees the rights of the people.

Explore and Discuss

You have described the event known as "the shot heard 'round the world." Now that you have finished the chapter, think again about that phrase. It comes from a poem written by Ralph Waldo Emerson in 1837. Why do you think Emerson used that phrase?

> Answers may vary, but should include the idea that the American Revolution inspired revolutions around the world.

Day 3

Asking the Tough Questions!

> Answers may vary.

Name _____ Date _____

Lesson Assessment Answer Key

The World Turned Upside Down: The American Revolution, Part 2

Answers:

1. In a short paragraph, give two reasons why most colonists had a positive attitude toward Britain in 1763.

    Scoring: Award one point for each correct reason, for a total of two points.

    o   because they had just helped defeat Britain's longtime rival, France, in the French and Indian War
    o   because they took pride in their English heritage
    o   because they enjoyed their rights and freedoms as Englishmen

2. In a short paragraph, summarize why the colonists opposed paying British taxes.

    Answer: Answers may vary but the student should include the following information:

    o   because most colonial assemblies, which were elected by colonists, held the "power of the purse"
    o   because they believed there should be no taxation without representation

Learning Coach Guide
Lesson 2: The French Revolution

Lesson Objectives

- Summarize Enlightenment ideas that promoted revolution in France.
- Describe the reigns of absolute monarchs in France.
- Describe the social structure of France and its influence on French life.
- Summarize the circumstances and events that led to the French Revolution.
- Compare the Declaration of the Rights of Man with the Declaration of Independence.
- Explain the revolutionaries' criticisms of the Church.
- Describe the events of the Reign of Terror.
- Recognize reforms made by the National Convention.
- Explain how Napoleon came to power.
- Identify major positions of the political spectrum.

PREPARE

Approximate lesson time is 60 minutes.

Materials

For the Student

- 💻 Declaration of the Rights of Man
- 💻 Lesson Answer Key
- 💻 Reading Guide
- 💻 The French Revolution: What Happened and When

    The Human Odyssey, Volume 2 edited by Klee, Cribb, and Holdren

    History Journal

Keywords and Pronunciation

Bastille (bah-STEEL)

dauphin (doh-FAN)

guillotine (GIH-luh-teen)

Liberté, égalité, fraternité (lee-behr-TAY, ay-ga-lee-TAY, fra-tehr-nee-TAY)

Maximilien Robespierre (mahk-see-meel-yan ROHBZ-pyehr)

Napoleon Bonaparte (nuh-POHL-yuhn BOH-nuh-pahrt)

Vive l' assemblée (veev lah-sahm-blay)

Vive la république (veev lah ray-poob-leek)

TEACH
Activity 1: The French Revolution (Offline)
Instructions
Activity 1. The French Revolution (Offline)

This lesson is designed to be completed in **3** class sessions.

Day 1
Read
Your student will read Chapter 2, from the beginning to "Storming the Bastille and Starting a Revolution," pages 368–374, and complete **Day 1** of the Reading Guide. When your student has finished, she should use the Lesson Answer Key to check her work, and then place the Reading Guide in her History Journal.

That's Class!
Your student will learn that French society was divided into three classes, or estates, and that the "common people" of France had little power compared to the nobles or the clergy. Your student will learn more about the estates by going online to assign members of French society to the proper estate.

Day 2
Read
Your student will read Chapter 2, from "Storming the Bastille and Starting a Revolution" to "Terror and Equality," pages 374–380, and complete **Day 2** of the Reading Guide. When your student has finished, she should use the Lesson Answer Key to check her work, and then place the Reading Guide in her History Journal.

Declaring the Rights of Man and the Citizen
Your student will learn that the deputies of the Third Estate formed the National Assembly and seized power. She will see how the National Assembly drafted a Declaration of the Rights of Man and will compare this document to America's Declaration of Independence by answering questions on the Declaration of the Rights of Man sheet.

Day 3
Read
Your student will read Chapter 2, from "Terror and Equality" to the end, pages 380–383, and complete **Day 3** of the Reading Guide. When your student has finished, she should use the Lesson Answer Key to check her work, and then place the Reading Guide in her History Journal.

What Happened and When?
Your student will assign dates to the most significant events in the French Revolution, arrange the events in chronological order, then complete a chart on The French Revolution: What Happened and When sheet.

A Spectrum of Political Opinion
Your student will learn about the political spectrum and then go online to figure out how the various movements and events of the French Revolution fit within the political spectrum.

ASSESS
Lesson Assessment: The French Revolution (*Online*)

Students will complete an online assessment based on the lesson objectives. The assessment will be scored by the computer. The attached answer key is the most current and may not coincide with previously printed guides.

TEACH
Activity 2. Optional: The French Revolution (*Online*)

The French Revolution

Day 1

Read

Reading Guide

1. Name two of the Enlightenment ideas that promoted revolution in France.
    people have natural rights; government should represent the people; rights should be written in a constitution

2. What kind of power did France's absolute monarchs possess?
    they had almost unlimited powers; they were all-powerful

3. Name the three estates into which French society was divided. Who were the members of each of the three estates?
    the First Estate (clergy); the Second Estate (nobles); the Third Estate ("commoners")

4. Look closely at the cartoon on page 371. Describe in your own words what it is trying to say.
    The "commoners" are carrying the nobles and the clergy; the Third Estate supports the other two estates; commoners are the only ones in society who do any real work; nobles and clergy are lazy

5. True or false? It was easy for a "commoner" to change his estate by acquiring wealth.
    false

6. Why did Louis XVI call a meeting of the Estates-General in 1789? How long had it been since such a meeting had been called?
    He needed money. The Estates-General had not met for 175 years.

7. One of the advantages of the First and Second Estates is that their members did not have to pay <u>taxes</u>.

8. Unfair taxes angered members of the Third Estate. But what would have happened if the Third Estate had tried to get the First and Second Estates to pay taxes? How would the estates have voted in the Estates-General?
    The First and Second Estates would have voted against the Third Estate.

9. If the Third Estate would be constantly outvoted, two to one, by the other two estates, how could commoners ever hope to gain a fairer share of power?
    by ending the Estates General and its division of people into estates; by having people vote instead of having estates vote

10. Deputies of the Third Estate took the <u>Tennis Court</u> Oath, swearing not to disband until they had drafted a new constitution.

11. What was the new name the deputies gave themselves?
    the National Assembly

Day 2

Read

Reading Guide

12. After the formation of the National Assembly, the Paris mob decided to get in on the action by storming the <u>Bastille</u>.

13. What was the mob hoping to find in this building? What did they find?
    arms and ammunition, prisoners; just seven prisoners

14. True or false? The new National Assembly wanted to immediately get rid of the monarchy completely.
    false

15. American revolutionaries drew up a Declaration of Independence. What kind of declaration did the French write?
    the Declaration of the Rights of Man

16. Why did the revolutionaries dislike the Church? Give at least two reasons.
    It was too wealthy; it was too powerful; religion ran contrary to reason.

Declaration of the Rights of Man

1. Declaration of Independence

2. Supreme Being

3. Enlightenment

4. John Locke; *philosophes*

5. liberty, property, security, resistance to oppression

6. powers

7. Answers may vary but could include: Frenchmen fighting on the side of the Americans had seen that royal power could be broken; they learned about the ideas that inspired the American Revolution; Lafayette returned to France with ideas about liberty

8. Answers may vary but could include references to constitutional monarchy, the Glorious Revolution in England, the writings of Locke about the exercise of power beyond right, the divine right of kings, particular behavior of particular kings

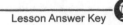

Day 3

Read

Reading Guide

17. What was the Reign of Terror?
    It was the period during the revolution when thousands of citizens were executed because they had been labeled (often wrongly) as enemies of the revolution.

18. Among the reforms of the National Convention were free <u>primary education</u> for all boys and girls, equal <u>inheritance</u> for both sons and daughters, and the abolition of <u>slavery</u> in the French colonies.

19. To whom did the Directors turn for help against their enemies? Why did they think that he could help them?
    Napoleon; he had an army and they thought they could control him

20. Napoleon took control of France by seizing <u>power</u> from the Directory. Soon he wielded as much power as a <u>dictator</u>.

21. If moderates had maintained control of the revolution, how do you think it would have turned out? If reactionaries had seized control, what would they have done?
    If the moderates had maintained control, it would have turned into a constitutional monarchy. If the reactionaries had seized control, there would have been a return to the days of absolute monarchs.

Thinking Cap Question:

Was there anything poor Louis XVI could have done to stop the revolution, to maintain the monarchy, or even to save his own head? Or, by 1789 was there nothing the king could have done?
    Answer could include that he could have: lived more frugally, avoided calling the Estates-General, sided with the Third Estate, embraced the constitution, not tried to flee France
    Or there was nothing he could have done, because of the demands for change by the Third Estate, the poverty of the people, the reactionary positions of the First and Second Estates.

What Happened and When?

    Spring 1789: The Estates-General meets.
    June 20, 1789: Members of the National Assembly take the Tennis Court Oath.
    July 14, 1789: Paris mob storms the Bastille.
    August 1789: The National Assembly issues the Declaration of the Rights of Man.
    October 1789: Parisians move the royal family from Versailles to the capital.
    August 1792: Paris mob imprisons the royal family.
    September 1792: Convention declares France a republic.
    January 21, 1793: King Louis XVI is executed.
    Spring 1793: Robespierre begins to rule France like a tyrant during the Reign of Terror.
    October 16, 1793: Marie Antoinette is executed.
    July 28, 1794: Robespierre's execution brings the Directory to power.
    1799: Napoleon Bonaparte seizes power from the Directory.

Learning Coach Guide
Lesson 3: Napoleon: From Revolution to Empire

Lesson Objectives

- Recognize the effects of Napoleon's rule on Europe.
- Summarize the major steps in Napoleon's rise to power.
- Describe Napoleon's reforms and their significance to the people of France.
- Explain how Napoleon was able to finance wars and win territory.
- Describe the Continental System and the consequences of imposing the system.
- Explain the reasons for Napoleon's invasion of Russia and his failure to defeat Russia.
- Summarize the events that led to Napoleon's final defeat at Waterloo.
- Identify on a map major physical and political features of Europe.

PREPARE

Approximate lesson time is 60 minutes.

Materials
For the Student

- 🖳 Europe's Changing Face
- 🖳 Napoleon: Hero or Tyrant?
- 🖳 Opinions
- 🖳 Reading Guide
- 🖳 Say What?

  The Human Odyssey, Volume 2 edited by Klee, Cribb, and Holdren

  History Journal

For the Adult

- 🖳 Europe's Changing Face Answer Key
- 🖳 Lesson Answer Key
- 🖳 Say What? Answer Key

TEACH
Activity 1: Napoleon: From Revolution to Empire (Offline)

Instructions

Activity 1. Napoleon: From Revolution to Empire (Offline)

This lesson is designed to be completed in 4 class sessions.

Day 1

Read

Your student will read Chapter 3, from the beginning to "Catastrophe in Russia," pages 384–394, and complete Day 1 of the Reading Guide. When your student has finished, she should use the Lesson Answer Key to check her work, and then place the Reading Guide in her History Journal.

That's Your Opinion!

Your student will pretend to be a member of the Third Estate and react to what Napoleon did. Napoleon was a man of action, who did some things that were good for France and its revolution—and some things that were not. The emperor stirred intense opinions among the French people. Over time, some of those who supported him may have started to question the wisdom of his actions.

Day 2

Read

Your student will read Chapter 3, from "Catastrophe in Russia" to the end, pages 394–399, and complete Day 2 of the Reading Guide. When your student has finished, she should use the Lesson Answer Key to check her work, and then place the Reading Guide in her History Journal.

Putting Napoleon on the Map

Your student will fill the Europe's Changing Face sheet to show how Napoleon transformed the map of Europe and how the powers that eventually defeated Napoleon redrew that map at the Congress of Vienna. In addition, your student will learn about the physical geography of Europe and its relevance to the life and conquests of Napoleon.

Day 3

"Say What?"

Your student will read a series of quotations by or about Napoleon, consider their meaning, and place them in the context of Napoleon's career. He will then choose the quotation that reveals the most about Napoleon.
Political Cartoons—Seriously Funny
Your student will go online to research political cartoons.

Day 4

Have Fun with Napoleon: Making Political Cartoons

Your student will take what he has learned from the chapter and the earlier activities—and design two political cartoons on the Napoleon: Hero or Tyrant? sheet. One cartoon should show Napoleon as hero of the revolution and the other cartoon should show him as a tyrant.

ASSESS

Lesson Assessment: Napoleon: From Revolution to Empire (*Online*)

Students will complete an online assessment based on the lesson objectives. The assessment will be scored by the computer. The attached answer key is the most current and may not coincide with previously printed guides.

Name _____   Date _____

Say What? Answer Key

Napoleon left us many memorable quotations. And much has been said about him. Explain each of the quotations below—is it something Napoleon said? Or something said about him? What does it mean? Why might Napoleon or someone else have said it? Does the quotation favor Napoleon? The first has been done for you.

At the end, complete the "Napoleon in a Nutshell" section.

"I am the Revolution."

Who: Napoleon

Meaning: Napoleon said this about his own role; it justified his all-powerful position.

Favorable? Most people today would say it is not favorable.

"My forces are three times greater than yours."

Who: Napoleon said it to Tsar Alexander in 1812, prior to the invasion of Russia.

Meaning: He was confident and intimidating.

Favorable? Answers may vary.

"You have won battles without cannon, crossed rivers without bridges, made forced marches without shoes…"

Who: Napoleon said it to his army.

Meaning: Napoleon was praising the troops of the Italian Campaign, 1796.

Favorable? Answers may vary.

"If you wish to be a success in the world, promise everything, deliver nothing."

Who: Napoleon said it.

Meaning: Success requires words but not results.

Favorable? Answers may vary.

"the little corporal"

Who: Others said it.

Meaning: name used by troops of the Italian campaign for their beloved commander

Favorable? Answers may vary.

"Enemy and Disturber of the Tranquility of the World"

Who: Others said it.

Meaning: Napoleon's actions and ideas disturbed the status quo.

Favorable? Answers may vary.

"Vive l'Empereur!"

Who: Others said it.

Meaning: "Long live the emperor!" (cries of the crowd after Napoleon's 1804 coronation as emperor in Notre Dame Cathedral)

Favorable? Answers may vary.

"soldier of the Revolution"

Who: Napoleon said it.

Meaning: His self-assessment of his rise through the ranks during the early days of the Revolution

Favorable? Answers may vary.

Say What?

Napoleon in a Nutshell

Choose your favorite quotation about Napoleon and explain why it best sums up the nature of the man.

Quotation: <u>Answers may vary.</u>

_____

What it tells us about Napoleon: <u>Could include observations about Napoleon's boldness, daring,</u>

<u>egoism, self-delusion, military genius, pride.</u>

_____

Name _____   Date _____

Europe's Changing Face Answer Key

1. Consulting the maps on pages 392 and 393 and the atlas at the back of the textbook, label the following on your map:

France	Kingdom of Italy	Britain
Austrian Empire	Spain	Prussia
Portugal	Sweden	Germany
Russian Empire	Holland	

Label the following cities:

Paris	Moscow	Waterloo	Vienna

Label the following physical features:

Alps	English Channel	Northern European Plain

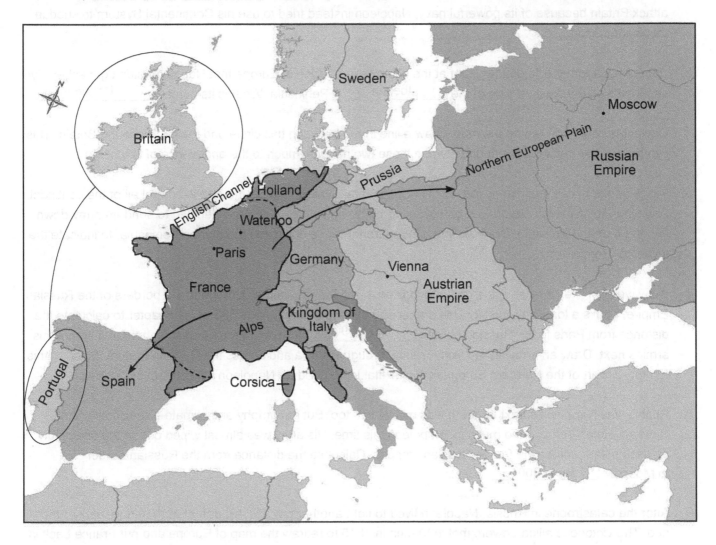

Name _____   Date _____

Europe's Changing Face Answer Key

2. Napoleon's first foreign victory was in _____Italy_____. Look at the map in the Atlas at the back of your textbook. What physical feature, or barrier, stands between France and this country? _____the Alps_____ If you need a clue, take another look at the first picture in this chapter.

3. But geography couldn't slow Napoleon for long. He went on to win great victories on battlefields all over Europe. Now we're going to see just how successful Napoleon was. Use a pencil or marker to indicate the extent of the French Empire in 1812, then color the empire light blue or light purple if you have it, like the map on pages 392–393. (Consider to be within the empire the "allies of France" indicated in the map legend.)

4. Quite an empire, huh? But he didn't get all of Europe. Circle Britain in red on the map. What makes it different from the other countries of Europe? What separates Britain from France? Britain is an _____island_____, separated from France and its all-conquering Napoleon by the _____English Channel_____. Unable to attack Britain because of its powerful navy, Napoleon instead tried to use his Continental System to subdue the island nation.

5. But there's another little country right at the southwestern edge of Europe that Napoleon didn't get either. You see it? It's on the western side of the _____Iberian_____ Peninsula. What is its name? _____Portugal_____

    Circle this country in red on the map. Draw a line in red between this circle and the circle around Britain. This symbolizes the trade that went on between these two nations, much to the annoyance of Napoleon.

6. Yes, Napoleon was really annoyed. For his Continental System to work, he had to control all of the continent. And when the Spanish began to break away from French control, Napoleon decided to send an army down into the Iberian Peninsula. Draw an arrow in red from France down into the Iberian Peninsula, to indicate the invading French army.

7. Now we (just like Napoleon) are going to look east—all the way across Europe to the borders of the Russian Empire. That's a long way, isn't it? Use a ruler and the scale bar on page 393 of the chapter to calculate the distance from Paris to the Russian border: _____about 900_____ miles. That's where Napoleon marched his armies next. Draw an arrow in red from France through Prussia and across the Russian frontier. Much of this territory is part of the Northern European Plain—flat land, good for Napoleon's quick-moving armies.

8. Russia was Napoleon's next target. It was mainly flat, too. But geography and climate—specifically, the Russian winter—proved too much for Napoleon this time. His army was almost wiped out on the seemingly endless march across the frozen Russian steppes. Calculate the distance from the Russian border to Moscow: _____about 600_____ miles.

9. After the catastrophe in Russia, Napoleon lived to fight another day. But his defeat at Waterloo marked the end. The victorious allied powers met in Vienna in 1815 to redraw the map of Europe and put France back in its place. To see how far they shrunk Napoleon's once-great realm, use a black marker and trace around the faint, dashed line on the map. This was France in 1815.

Napoleon: From Revolution to Empire

Day 1

Read

Reading Guide

1. Napoleon was born on the Mediterranean island of <u>Corsica</u> and later lived in the French capital, <u>Paris</u>.

2. Napoleon the soldier gained political power by first gaining military power. He rose through the ranks of the <u>army</u> at the beginning of the Revolution. He helped put down a <u>royalist</u> uprising in Paris. And he took command of a new French army in <u>Italy</u>.

3. How did Napoleon rise from first consul to emperor?
   He dominated the other consuls and had himself made consul for life. Then he had his collaborators proclaim him emperor.

4. Name three reforms Napoleon made that improved the lives of the people of France.
   Answers may vary but should include at least three of the following: a civil service system that rewarded talent; improved sidewalk, sewers, and water supply in Paris; a unified legal system; new markets and quays along the Seine; a new system of roads; new theaters; an efficient postal service; improved schools

5. How did Napoleon raise soldiers for his army?
   mandatory military service, citizen soldiers

6. What was the name of the North American territory that Napoleon sold to the United States to help pay for his wars?
   Louisiana

7. To attack the island of Britain, Napoleon had to cross the <u>English Channel</u>.

8. To defeat Britain, Napoleon devised the <u>Continental</u> System, which banned Europeans from buying and selling with the (trade-dependent) island nation.

9. Name one country from southwestern Europe that refused to participate in the Continental System.
   Portugal, Spain

10. Portugal and Spain make up the <u>Iberian</u> Peninsula.

That's _Your_ Opinion!
   Answers may vary.

Day 2

Read

Reading Guide

11. Which other (huge) country also tried to break away from the Continental System?
    Russia

12. When the Royal Navy defeated the French fleet, Napoleon marched his army all the way across Europe to invade <u>Russia</u>.

13. To build up his enormous army for the invasion of Russia, Napoleon raised soldiers from <u>the conquered territories</u> as well as from France.

14. True or false? Napoleon invaded Russia because the Russians would not let Napoleon put his brother on the Russian throne.
    false

15. Napoleon made it all the way to the Russian capital. What is the name of that city?
    Moscow

16. What strategy did the Russians use to defeat Napoleon?
    They refused to meet the French in battle. Instead, they retreated before the advancing invaders, burning their own villages and fields to prevent the French from finding food and supplies.

17. Napoleon escaped from the island of <u>Elba</u>, raised an <u>army</u> in Paris, and tried to defeat the <u>British</u> before the Prussians arrived on the field of battle.

18. Napoleon gave the conquered peoples of Europe a unified legal system know as the <u>Napoleonic Code</u>. However, many Europeans resented being ruled by Napoleon, whom they regarded as a <u>tyrant</u>.

19. After defeating Napoleon, the allies redrew the border of Europe at a congress, or meeting, of their leaders. In which European city was the congress held?
    Vienna

Explore and Discuss

History is full of "what ifs." What if Napoleon had been defeated in Italy? What if the Continental System had worked? What if the French had won the battle of Trafalgar? What if the Prussians had been delayed at Waterloo?

Consider these questions:

1. What if Napoleon had never been born? (In what ways would history have been different? Do you think someone else would have done what Napoleon did? Why?)
   Answers may vary.

2. The French Revolution began as a struggle for the rights of the people against a single ruler with all the power. It ended by giving all power to another single ruler. Why do you think that happened?
   Answers may vary.

Learning Coach Guide
Lesson 4. Optional: Your Choice

PREPARE

Approximate lesson time is 60 minutes.

Learning Coach Guide
Lesson 5: Latin American Independence Movements

Lesson Objectives

- Describe the social and political structure of Latin American colonies in 1800.
- Identify significant leaders of nineteenth century Latin American independence movements and their accomplishments and failings.
- Explain why attempts to establish republics in Latin America were less successful than in the United States.
- Identify major physical, political, and cultural features of Latin America.

PREPARE

Approximate lesson time is 60 minutes.

Materials

For the Student

- Ask the Revolutionary
- Mapping Out Latin America
- Off the Charts!
- Reading Guide

The Human Odyssey, Volume 2 edited by Klee, Cribb, and Holdren

History Journal

For the Adult

- Lesson Answer Key
- Mapping Out Latin America Answer Key

Keywords and Pronunciation

caudillos (kaw-DEEL-yohs) : military strongmen who seized power in South American nations after their liberation from Spain

Dolores (doh-LOH-res)

Francisco de Miranda (fran-SEES-koh day mee-RAHN-dah)

Ignacio Allende (uh-YEN-day)

José de San Martín (hoh-SAY day san mahr-TEEN)

Miguel Hidalgo y Costilla (mee-GEHL ee-DAHL-goh ee kahs-TEE-yah)

Querétaro (kay-RAY-tah-roh)

Rio de Janeiro (REE-oh day zhuh-NER-oh)

Simón Bolívar (see-MOHN buh-LEE-vahr)

TEACH
Activity 1: Latin American Independence Movements *(Offline)*
Instructions
Activity 1. Latin American Independence Movements (Offline)

This lesson is designed to be completed in **3** class sessions.

Day 1
Read
Your student will read Chapter 4, from the beginning to "San Martín, Hero of the South," pages 400–406, and complete **Day 1** of the Reading Guide. When your student has finished, he should use the Lesson Answer Key to check his work, and then place the Reading Guide in his History Journal.

Mapping Out Latin America
Your student will learn about the geography of Latin America by completing a map.

Day 2
Read
Your student will read Chapter 3, from "San Martín, Hero of the South" to the end, pages 406–415, and complete **Day 2** of the Reading Guide. When your student has finished, he should use the Lesson Answer Key to check his work, and then place the Reading Guide in his History Journal.

Charting Latin America's Leaders
Your student will fill in a chart on the main leaders of the Latin American independence movements—Miranda, Bolívar, San Martín, and Hidalgo.

Day 3
The Revolutionary Americas
Your student will learn how the revolutions in Latin America differed from the American Revolution that gave birth to the United States by completing an online activity.

Ask the Revolutionary
Your student will pretend to interview each of Latin America's major revolutionaries about his struggle to win independence.

Assessment (On/Offline)
After he has completed the **Day 3** activities, your student will take the Lesson Assessment.

ASSESS

Lesson Assessment: Latin American Independence Movements, Part 1

(*Online*)

Students will complete an online assessment based on the lesson objectives. The assessment will be scored by the computer. The attached answer key is the most current and may not coincide with previously printed guides.

Lesson Assessment: Latin American Independence Movements, Part 2

(*Offline*)

Students will complete this part of the Lesson Assessment offline. Print the test and have students complete it on their own. Use the answer key to score the test, and then enter the results online. The attached answer key is the most current and may not coincide with previously printed guides.

Name _____   Date _____

Mapping Out Latin America Answer Key

1. Latin America
(Red Pencil)

2. South America
(Green Pencil)

3. Mexico

4. Gulf of Mexico

4. Caribbean Sea

8. Caracas

7. Venezuela

6. Orinoco River

4. Pacific Ocean

7. Colombia

7. Ecuador

7. Peru

6. Amazon River

8. Lima

7. Brazil

5. Andes

8. Rio de Janeiro

7. Chile

8. Buenos Aires

7. Argentina

4. Atlantic Ocean

1. On the map, draw a line in red pencil around Latin America.

2. With a green pencil, draw a line around South America.

3. Which major Latin American country lies north of South America? Label it on the map.

4. Latin America is bordered by four bodies of water. Label them.

5. A range of mountains runs the length of South America, along the western coast. Indicate the mountain range with a series of mountain symbols (^^^^^^) and label the range.

6. Trace the course of two of South America's important rivers—the Amazon River and the Orinoco River. Label the rivers.

7. Add the following country labels:

Venezuela	Colombia	Brazil	Argentina
Chile	Peru	Ecuador	

8. Add the following city labels:

Caracas	Rio de Janeiro	Buenos Aires	Lima

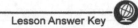

Latin American Independence Movements

Day 1

Read

Reading Guide

1. Settlers in the colonies of Latin America belonged to different classes. *Peninsulares* were <u>Spanish-born officials who carried out the king's will</u>.

2. Creoles formed another class of people in the Latin American colonies. *Creoles* were <u>colonists born in Latin America</u>.

3. What is a *mestizo*? (If you do not remember, see page 254.)
    A mestizo is a person of mixed race descended from a Spaniard and an Indian (such as an Aztec or an Inca).

4. Latin America stretches all the way from the <u>southern border of the United States</u> in the north to the tip of <u>South America</u> in the south.

5. Latin America is so named because the majority of the people there speak <u>Spanish</u> or <u>Portuguese</u>, both of which developed from Latin.

6. One of the early leaders of the Latin American independence movements was Francisco de <u>Miranda</u>. He learned much about political freedom when he visited <u>the United States</u>.

7. Miranda was chosen by <u>Simón Bolívar</u> to lead an uprising against Spanish rule in <u>Venezuela</u>.

8. Bolívar eagerly read Enlightenment writers such as <u>Locke, Voltaire,</u> and <u>Montesquieu</u>.

9. True or false? Miranda's uprising against the Spanish was successful.
    False

10. Miranda spent his last years in <u>a dungeon, in prison in Spain</u>.

11. Eventually, Bolívar led a revolutionary army that freed Venezuela, whose people hailed him with the Spanish title <u>El Libertador</u>, which in English means <u>The Liberator</u>.

Day 2

Read

12. In which South American country was José de San Martín regarded as the greatest hero?
    Argentina

13. San Martín led a rebel army across the <u>Andes</u> mountains, from Argentina to <u>Chile</u>.

14. Who was the Chilean with the Irish family name who became the first leader of his liberated nation?
    Bernardo O'Higgins

15. Of all their colonies in South America, the Spanish prized <u>Peru</u> above the rest. After San Martín helped liberate it, he ruled it as <u>Protector of Peru</u>.

16. True or false? Bolívar believed that the people of Peru were ready to rule themselves and did not need strong leadership.
    False

17. True or false? Bolívar hoped to form a large nation covering much of South America.
    True

18. Latin Americans often faced political chaos after winning their liberation. This allowed <u>political</u> <u>strongmen or caudillos</u> to rise to power.

19. The people of the new Latin American nations did not have a history of electing their own representatives, passing laws, or charting their own future. That's why attempts to establish <u>republics</u> in Latin America were less successful than in the <u>United States</u>.

20. What was the largest colony in South America and what language did the colonists there speak?
    Brazil; Portuguese

21. When Brazil declared its independence, it was a <u>kingdom or monarchy</u>, unlike the Spanish-speaking colonies, which became republics.

22. This colonist led a rebellion against Spanish rule. The Spanish captured and executed him. But he is remembered as the father of Mexican independence. Who was he?
    Miguel Hidalgo y Costilla (Father Hidalgo)

23. The father of Mexican independence was not a military leader or a political figure. Instead, he was a <u>priest</u>.

24. Mexico dates its independence to the day on which Father Hidalgo <u>rang the church bell</u> and gave the cry that sparked a revolution.

25. Three large bodies of water border Latin America. To the west is the <u>Pacific</u> Ocean, to the East is the <u>Atlantic</u> Ocean, and to the northeast is the <u>Caribbean</u> Sea.

26. True or false? The Alps run down the east coast of South America.
    False

Explore and Discuss

Now that you've learned about revolutions and liberation movements in both North and South America, consider these questions:

What characteristics did colonies and liberation movements in the United States and Latin America share?
    The North American and Latin American peoples both wanted to win their freedom from European kings; both faced resistance to their desire for freedom; both had to raise armies to fight for their liberation; both had great liberation leaders, such as George Washington and Simón Bolívar, who are still revered today.

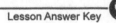

In what ways were the colonies and liberation movements in these two parts of the Americas different?
　　The North American colonies managed to unite to form a single nation; Latin America splintered into
　　many different nations. The United States was able to maintain a representative democracy for its free
　　citizens; in Latin America, many of the citizens fell under the rule of military strongmen. For three hundred
　　years, the Spanish had exercised strict royal control over their colonies; in North America, the colonies
　　under British rule had exercised a lot of self-rule.

Charting Latin America's Leaders

Off the Charts!

	Miranda	Bolívar	San Martín	Hidalgo
Creole or peninsulare?	creole	creole	creole	creole
Born in	Venezuela	Venezuela	Argentina	Mexico
Family background	son of wealthy merchant	son of rich aristocrat	mother from Spanish nobility, father a high-ranking colonial official	the son of a middle class creole who ran a hacienda, or ranch
Before becoming a revolutionary	captain in royal army	one of richest people in Venezuela	Spanish army officer	provincial creole priest
Sources of ideas, inspiration	read philosophical works about freedom as natural right; discussions with Jefferson, Madison, Paine in U.S.	traveled to Spain; read Enlightenment thinkers such as Locke, Voltaire, Montesquieu	spent weeks in London discussing revolutions in South America	studied works of Enlightenment philosophers; admired ideas of French Revolution

	Miranda	Bolívar	San Martín	Hidalgo
Goals in own words	"the liberty and independence of the entire Spanish-American continent"	"I will not rest, not in body or soul, till I have broken the chains of Spain"	"the prompt conclusion of the war [and] the organization of the different republics"	"recover from the hated Spaniards the land stolen...300 years ago"
Territory tried to liberate	Venezuela	Venezuela, Colombia, Peru	Argentina, Chile, Peru	Mexico
Difficulties	army poorly trained, ill equipped	troops loyal to Spain fought back, recovered liberated territory	had to lead army across Andes	disorderly revolutionary army
Major accomplishment	led early movement for liberation from Spanish rule	hailed by the people as "The Liberator"	served as Protector of Peru after it won its independence	revered as the father of Mexican independence

Ask the Revolutionary

Answers may vary, but could include some of the following information.

Francisco de Miranda, why did your attempt to liberate Venezuela fail so badly even though you had Bolívar's support?

> The Venezuelan rebel soldiers were poorly trained and ill-equipped. Many of the rebel officers disliked me because I had been in Europe for so many years; they treated me as if I were a stranger. Also, when an earthquake destroyed Caracas and some other rebel cities and only inflicted minor damage to the cities loyal to Spain, some said it was a sign from God.

Simón Bolívar, what was your greatest achievement?

> My greatest achievement was leading Colombian forces into Venezuela. Being hailed as "El Libertador" in Caracas, made me very proud.

And what was your bitterest disappointment?

> Miranda's failed rebellion was extremely disappointing. I was also very disappointed that I was unable to forge a single, large nation in South America. I became very unpopular when I persisted in trying to form one.

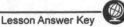

José de San Martín, you fought bravely for Spain in Europe. Why did you feel so strongly about freeing South America from Spanish rule?

> I was fed up with the Spanish prejudice against anyone born in the colonies. I encountered all kinds of revolutionary ideas when I spent some time in London. I came to believe that Spain's tight control of the colonies in America was wrong.

What was the toughest challenge you faced?

> I think the toughest challenge I faced was leading an army across the Andes from Argentina to Chile to drive the Spanish forces out of South America.

Miguel Hidalgo y Costilla, you are remembered as the father of Mexican independence. That's a great achievement, but looking back, is there anything you would have done differently?

> I wish I had tried to start the revolution when I was younger; I was an old man by the time the revolution began. I also would not have cried out, "Death to bad government!" because some of our followers thought I meant "Death to the Spaniards!" I would have tried to make sure the wealthy creoles joined our cause; unfortunately, many of them felt threatened. I wish I could have prevented the death of my friend, Captain Allende.

Name _____   Date _____

Lesson Assessment Answer Key
Latin American Independence Movements, Part 2

1. In a short paragraph, describe at least three reasons why new Latin American nations faced difficulties in establishing and maintaining new republics.

   Answers may vary, but should include three of the reasons listed in the following paragraph.

   The people of the new Latin American nations had no experience electing their own representatives, passing laws, or charting their own future. And they were unable to unite into a single nation. Instead, they split into several different countries. Their leaders feared that they were not ready to govern themselves and worried about establishing republics. In the end, many of them fell under the rule of military strongmen instead of elected leaders.

   Give 2 points for each reason that is correctly described.

Enter the letter next to the correct answer in the Word Bank.

Word Bank
a. Francisco de Miranda
b. Father Hidalgo
c. Simón Bolívar
d. José de San Martín

2. Who became the Protector of Peru? __d.__

3. Who traveled to the United States and discussed his ideas with Thomas Jefferson, James Madison, and Thomas Paine? __a.__

4. Who led a rebel army across the Andes from Argentina to Chile? __d.__

5. Who surrendered to the Spanish when he was commanding the Venezuelan rebel army and spent his last years in a Spanish dungeon? __a.__

6. Who did the people of Venezuela hail as El Libertador—The Liberator? __c.__

7. Who became Argentina's greatest hero? __d.__

8. Who was known as the father of Mexican independence? __b.__

Learning Coach Guide
Lesson 6: The Russia of the Romanovs

Lesson Objectives

- Describe how Russia differed from western Europe in the sixteenth and seventeenth centuries and explain why.
- Describe the social structure of Russian society.
- Identify Peter the Great.
- Locate on a map the city of St. Petersburg and the boundaries of Russia.
- Recognize the significance of warm water ports for Russia.
- Identify Catherine the Great.
- Describe the lives of Russia's serfs.
- Identify Alexander I.
- Describe the Decembrist Uprising.

PREPARE

Approximate lesson time is 60 minutes.

Materials

For the Student

- 🖳 Class-Conscious Russia
- 🖳 Reading Guide
- 🖳 Water, Water Everywhere
- 🖳 What's So Great?

The Human Odyssey, Volume 2 edited by Klee, Cribb, and Holdren

History Journal

For the Adult

- 🖳 Lesson Answer Key
- 🖳 Water, Water Everywhere--Answer Key
- 🖳 Water, Water Everywhere Answer Key

Keywords and Pronunciation

Caucasus (KAW-kuh-suhs)

Cossacks : wild-looking Russian cavalrymen

Crimea (kriy-MEE-uh) : large peninsula on the Black Sea

Hermitage : Catherine the Great's residence, which became a center of culture and a great art museum

TEACH
Activity 1: The Russia of the Romanovs (Offline)
Instructions
Activity 1. The Russia of the Romanovs (Offline)

This lesson is designed to be completed in **4** class sessions.

Day 1
Read

Your student will read Chapter 5, from the beginning to "Serfdom Endures and Expands," pages 416–423, and complete **Day 1** of the Reading Guide. When your student has finished, he should use the Lesson Answer Key to check his work, and then place the Reading Guide in his History Journal.

Water, Water Everywhere

Your student will learn about the geography of Russia, particularly its long coastlines and ports by filling out the Water, Water Everywhere sheet.

Class-Conscious Russia

Your student will learn about the different social classes that made up the Russia of the Romanovs by filling out the Class-Conscious Russia sheet.

Day 2
Read

Your student will read Chapter 5, from "Serfdom Endures and Expands" to the end, pages 423–429, and complete **Day 2** of the Reading Guide. When your student has finished, he should use the Lesson Answer Key to check his work, and then place the Reading Guide in his History Journal.

Mapping the Growth of an Empire

Your student will complete an online map activity to learn about the growth of the Russian Empire.

What's So Great About the Romanovs?

By pretending to interview the tsars, your student will learn about the greatest achievements of Peter, Catherine, and Alexander—and also their worst failing.

Day 3
Two Time Lines

Your student will learn about the key events in Russian political history—and compare when they took place with major developments in Europe and the Americas.

Field Trip: Visiting St. Petersburg and Its Hermitage Museum

Your student will go online to see the sights of the city and its famous museum.

Day 4
Assessment (On/Offline)

After he has completed the **Day 3** activities, your student will take the Lesson Assessment.

ASSESS

Lesson Assessment: The Russia of the Romanovs, Part 1 (*Online*)

Students will complete an online assessment based on the lesson objectives. The assessment will be scored by the computer. The attached answer key is the most current and may not coincide with previously printed guides.

Lesson Assessment: The Russia of the Romanovs, Part 2 (*Offline*)

Students will complete this part of the Lesson Assessment offline. Print the test and have students complete it on their own. Use the answer key to score the test, and then enter the results online. The attached answer key is the most current and may not coincide with previously printed guides.

The Russia of the Romanovs

Day 1

Read

Reading Guide

1. Name two movements that had changed the Western world by the seventeenth century but had barely touched Russia.
    the Renaissance, Reformation, age of exploration

2. What practice or institution most differentiated Russia from the West?
    serfdom

3. Serfs were peasants who were bound by law to the <u>land</u> on which they worked.

4. Which tsar assumed the throne in 1689? What was his family name?
    Peter the Great, Romanov

5. Peter was a great reformer. In 1697 he set off on an 18-month tour of <u>western Europe</u>, the first Russian ruler to venture abroad during times of <u>peace</u>.

6. Name two of Peter's reforms.
    Answers may vary. He reformed the government and the Church. He promoted on the basis of merit not birth. He insisted on Western dress. He built roads, canals, and factories. He modernized the army.

7. Perhaps Peter's greatest achievement was the construction of a port on the Baltic Sea called <u>St. Petersburg</u>. His greatest failing was to leave unreformed the institution of <u>serfdom.</u>

8. In 1762 a German-born princess named Empress <u>Catherine</u> came to the throne. She promoted <u>Enlightenment or liberal</u> ideas and fostered the arts.

9. Catherine also modernized Russia. Name two of her reforms.
    She encouraged industry and trade with her European neighbors. She built roads. She improved education, especially for girls. She proposed a new code of laws.

10. In the end, however, Catherine did little to improve the lot of the vast majority of her subjects—the <u>serfs</u>.

Class-Conscious Russia

1. "My family ruled Russia for more than 300 years. I guess you could say that, just like my father and his father before him, I'm all-powerful. I have a special title. What is it?"
    tsar

2. "My family is bound to the land on which we work. We have as few rights as slaves. On official records, we are even listed as the property of those who own the fields we till. What are we known as?"
    serfs

3. "We are powerful and grand figures in Russia. We own much of the country's land. We grow our whiskers long, which is in keeping with Russian tradition. Sometimes we're called nobles, but we also have another, Russian name. What is it?"
   boyars

4. "I am the head of the Orthodox Church of Russia. The head of that Church has a unique name. What is it?"
   patriarch or patriarch of Moscow

5. "I am a poor man from the Russian countryside. I have a small plot of land with which I try to feed my family. What class do I belong to?"
   peasant

6. "I am a believer in the new ideas from Europe that are intended to liberate people from ignorance and backwardness. What am I known as?"
   a liberal

Day 2

Read

Reading Guide

11. Russia's serfs lived in single-room cabins made of <u>logs or clay</u>. They did not own the <u>land</u> upon which they toiled and possessed few <u>rights</u> under the law.

12. Name one of the ways in which a serf could "escape" the hardships of his life.
    Answers may vary, but could include: join the army, work in a factory, toil on one of the country's great construction projects

13. In 1801, Catherine the Great's grandson ascended the throne as <u>Alexander I</u>. She had always referred to her beloved grandson as <u>Monsieur Alexander</u>.

14. How did the new tsar delight Russian liberals when he assumed power?
    Answers may vary, but could include: lifting a ban on foreign books, reopening private publishing houses, freeing political prisoners, lifting a ban on foreign travel, or improving the education system

15. War with which country halted Alexander's plans to reform Russia?
    France

16. In the year <u>1812</u>, the Russians defeated the French emperor, <u>Napoleon</u>, and forced his army to retreat from the city of <u>Moscow</u>.

17. After Alexander died, revolutionaries launched a failed attempt to overthrow the Russian government. Their rebellion was known as the <u>Decembrist Uprising</u>.

Explore and Discuss

1. natural liberty, supreme good
2. the safety of every citizen, the equality of citizens
3. liberty
4. nature and reason

5. equals
6. innocent
7. house and family

Why, despite the efforts of these accomplished leaders, did serfdom prove so difficult to eliminate?
> Answers may vary but could include Russia's resistance to change, the need for Russian monarchs to keep the support of the boyars (who would not tolerate the abolition of serfdom), the economy's dependence on serfdom, the fear of change, or events elsewhere in Europe.

What's So Great About the Romanovs?

Peter the Great

Interviewer: Tsar Peter, how did your country differ from the rest of Europe and the Americas when you became tsar?
> Peter: Russia did not enjoy many of the benefits that had resulted from the scientific revolution, the Age of Exploration, the Renaissance, or the Reformation. Our country looked to the past much more than to the future. The attitude in Russia was "If it is old, it must be good. If it is new, it must be bad."

Interviewer: Why did you feel you had to travel to western Europe in 1697?
> Peter: I needed to travel there myself to find out how other, more modern European countries did things. I realized that people there had skills and crafts that we Russians did not possess. For Russia to grow, expand, and modernize, we needed to adopt western ways.

Interviewer: You have never been one to be bashful about your greatest achievements. What were they?
> Peter: Single-handedly, I dragged Russia into the modern era—by the force of my energies and my daring ambition. I made Russians work hard to bring about change. But no one worked harder to make this happen than I did myself. I'm proud of the way I expanded the country's borders and reorganized its government and Church. But if I had to pick one single achievement, I would have to say it was the construction of the great city of St. Petersburg.

Interviewer: And, if I may be so bold, Your Majesty, how about your greatest failure?
> Peter: I regret to say that my greatest failure was in not easing the burden of serfdom. That institution, more than anything else, tied Russia to its ignorant past.

Catherine the Great

Interviewer: Empress, history remembers you as Catherine the Great, one of Russia's most outstanding rulers. In what ways did you modernize Russia?
> Catherine: I introduced new ideas, particularly the ideas of the Enlightenment that were becoming so popular in France. I tried to attract the leading thinkers of the day to Russia and did my best to promote the arts. I also proposed a new code of laws, and modernized the country's industry, trade, and roads.

Interviewer: Your Majesty, you were a monarch who valued education highly. Why did you think education was so important for Russians?
> Catherine: As a single person, there was only so much I could do to change Russia. I did what I could. But to transform the country, more people needed to be educated—taught new and better ways of doing things, conducting themselves, and organizing society. This might seem like a slow way to bring about change, but in the long run I think it is the best way.

Interviewer: You like to be thought of as a new kind of Russian monarch, one inspired by the new ideas of the European Enlightenment. Why was it so difficult to make Enlightenment ideas work in Russia?

   Catherine: That brings us back to education—and the ignorance of the majority of the Russian people. Most Russian peasants knew little or nothing about the world beyond their farm or village. They did things as their parents, grandparents, and great grandparents had always done them. They believed that old ways were the best ways. The new ideas of the Enlightenment meant little to such people.

Interviewer: Why were you unable to end serfdom?

   Catherine: Again, because Russians resist change. Even an empress, regardless of how powerful she seems, can do little to change such an old institution. To be honest, though, I was in a difficult situation. I needed the support of the nobles to stay in power. And the nobles would not tolerate any moves to end serfdom. You could say, despite my best intentions, my hands were tied.

Alexander I

Interviewer: Your Majesty, you were the grandson of Catherine the Great. What can you tell me about your childhood and your early education?

   Alexander: Grandmother did everything she could to make sure I had a good upbringing and the best education. Education, as you may already know, was one of her top priorities. She made sure I had the best of tutors.

Interviewer: Monsieur Alexander, unlike some earlier leaders, you were never known as "the Great." But what do you consider your greatest achievement?

   Alexander: My greatest achievement is one that I shared with the people of Russia. In the great patriotic war against the French invaders—we defeated that awful Napoleon Bonaparte. The day I rode into Paris with the great liberating armies of Europe was the proudest day of my reign.

Interviewer: In later years, you changed your opinion about some of the new thinking that came out of France. Why did you change your mind?

   Alexander: Some of the ideas sounded fine in theory. But when they were put into practice, they were disastrous. Just look at what happened during the French Revolution: the church was persecuted, nobles fled the country, and the king and queen were executed. And then Napoleon came to power and unleashed war all across Europe. No, the new thinking that came out of France was just too dangerous.

Interviewer: Your Majesty, why were you unable to improve the lives of the majority of your subjects, the serfs?

   Alexander: Like my grandmother and others, I tried to make some changes. But when you are the tsar, things are never as simple as they seem. There was so much resistance to change. And to tell you the truth, I did get cold feet after I saw what happened in France after all that talk about liberty, equality, and fraternity. You just don't know where it's all going to stop.

Day 3

Two Time Lines

Answers may vary and should contain some of the following points.

Despite Setbacks, the West Outpaces Russia in Political, Social, and Scientific Arenas

   1350s–1600s: Russia changes very little while western Europe experiences the Renaissance and the Age of Exploration. Russia rarely embraces technological advances. Serfdom declines in Europe, but increases in Russia.

Early 1600s: Russia continues to be ruled by tsars, while the West questions the role of royalty and pushes for political reforms.

1776, 1789, 1790: As Americans issue the Declaration of Independence and the French revolt, the empress Catherine II introduces some reforms but quells the serfs' revolt in Russia.

1807, 1816: Britain abolishes the slave trade. Almost a decade later, Russia's tsar—Alexander I—orders a study to consider the abolition of serfdom.

Russia Modernizes and Westernizes

1698: Peter I launches a crusade to reform Russia by looking to more technologically advanced lands in the West. Peter tours Europe and recruits more than 800 European experts to go to Russia to help him modernize the country.

1703: Peter I founds the city of St. Petersburg, which becomes Russia's first warm-water port. This new capital provides access to the Baltic Sea and to the West. St. Petersburg opens up trade, which Peter considers his "window on the West."

1769: Catherine II opens the first girls' school. She enlarges the realm of Russia by winning the territory on the Crimea and expands the empire past the Caucasus Mountains. Empress Catherine II continues effort to modernize Russia by promoting education and European philosophy, art, and literature.

Russia and the West Progress but More Reform Needed

early 1600s : The British challenge the right of kings.

1700, 1776, 1789: Peter improves the army and introduces many new ideas and reforms but limits the power of the boyars. Revolutions in France and the Americas give the people greater political power. Empress Catherine II continues effort to modernize Russia by promoting education and European philosophy, art, and literature.

1800s Alexander I helps liberate Europe from Napoleon, but the majority of Russia's people remain enslaved as serfs.

1825 Russian army officers try to demand a constitutional government, but fail.

Name _____   Date _____

Water, Water Everywhere Answer Key

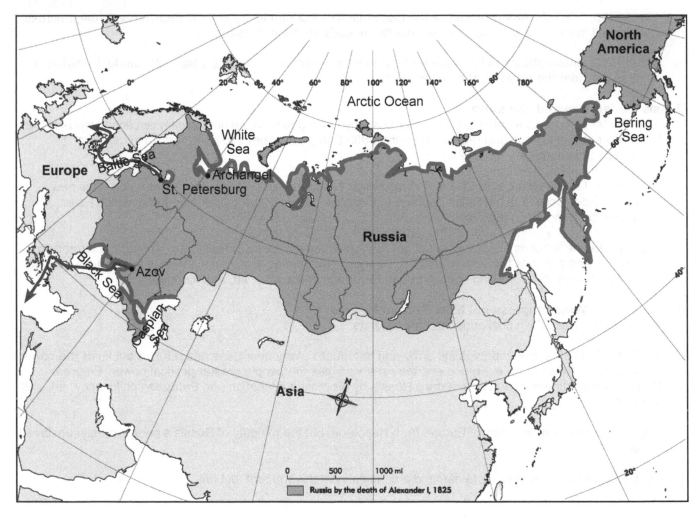

1. Take a good look at this map of Russia. What will immediately strike you is the size of the country; Russia was the biggest country in the world (as it still is today). It was also the country with the longest coastline in the world. Take a blue pencil and trace the various coastlines of mainland Russia. Using a ruler and the scale bar on the map, estimate the length of Russia's coastline. How long is it?

    Accept any reasonable estimate between 5,000 and 7,000 miles; it is very difficult to estimate inlets.

2. At about what latitude is the longest portion of Russia's coastline?   **70° N latitude**
    Name 3 other places in the world at that latitude.

    Answers could include Alaska, Northern Canada, Greenland, Norway, Sweden, Finland, Iceland

3. Label the following bodies of water. (Consult the map on page 418 of the chapter, if you need to).

Arctic Ocean	Bering Sea	Caspian Sea
Black Sea	Baltic Sea	White Sea

Water, Water Everywhere Answer Key

4. Wow! There are a lot of seas, aren't there? Now draw a dot on the map to indicate the location of the city of Archangel and then label it. It was Russia's only major port during the early part of Peter the Great's reign. Because this port is so far north, on the shores of the White Sea, it was frozen solid for six months of every year.

5. How do you think Russia's geography contributed to her lagging behind western Europe for so long?

   Russia's geography was significant in causing a lag in the country's development. Western Europe embraced new technologies and new political ideas earlier than Russia. Russia was a very large country which straddled Europe and Asia. Russia had few outlets to the sea and no ice-free seaports. These factors made trade and communication with western Europe difficult and, therefore, European innovations spread very slowly across Russia.

6. Peter was determined to gain more ports for Russia. Why did he need more ports? In general, what benefits would more ports confer on Russia? Answer the questions by writing a brief paragraph.

   Answers could include the following:
   Peter needed ports that could operate for more than six months a year. He needed ports that served different parts of the country, not just the north. More seaports would facilitate trade and contact with the other countries of Europe, which would help modernize Russia and increase the country's wealth and power.

7. Peter sent his army to fight the Turks and capture the port of Azov, which gave Russia access to the Black Sea. Draw a dot on the map to indicate the location of Azov and then label it. With a red pencil, draw an arrow from Azov through the Black Sea out into the Mediterranean Sea. It will show the route Russian ships began to take to reach the West.

8. Peter's armies also seized part of the Baltic coastline from the Swedes. There Peter built a new port city and capital for Russia—St. Petersburg. Draw a dot on the map to indicate the location of St. Petersburg and then label it. With a red pencil, draw an arrow from St. Petersburg through the Baltic Sea and out toward the rest of western Europe.

Lesson Assessment Answer Key

The Russia of the Romanovs, Part 2

Answers:

1. (15 points) Describe at least three ways in which Russia differed from western European countries in the 1600s and explain the reasons for those differences.

   Answers may vary, but should include three of the following points:

   Serfdom was widespread in Russia at a time when it was disappearing in the rest of Europe.
   Most Russians belonged to the Orthodox Church, which was different from the Catholic and Protestant churches of the rest of Europe.
   Many Russians dressed in traditional clothes that were different from those worn in the West.
   Men often wore long beards, which were no longer considered stylish in the rest of Europe.
   Russians used a different calendar.
   Russia was not affected by the Renaissance, the Reformation, or the Age of Exploration.
   In general, Russia was isolated and different because of its geography and its traditional culture that valued old ways more than modern ways.

   Award 5 points (for a total of 15 points) for each difference your student described correctly.

2. (12 points) Name at least three areas of Russian life that Peter the Great reformed or modernized and at least one area that he did not change significantly.

   Answers may vary, but should include three of the following points about reforms and one point about an area that was unchanged.

   Peter introduced technological advances that he had learned about during his travels.
   Peter reorganized Russia's government and the Russian Orthodox Church.
   Peter the Great introduced an official state currency, adopted England's calendar, ordered construction of new roadways, and opened new factories.
   Peter trained and equipped the army to fight more like western Europe armies.
   Peter expanded Russia's borders to include a warm-water port. His armies gained control of the port of Azov, which gave Russia access to the Black Sea. He gained access to the Baltic Sea by taking part of the Baltic coastline from the Swedes.
   Russia remained a feudal nation led by an all-powerful tsar. Peter did little to improve the life of Russia's serfs. He imposed new taxes on Russia's poor to finance wars and building projects. He spread serfdom to the lands he conquered.

   Award 3 points (for a total of 12 points) for each change your student described correctly.

Answer the following question by entering the letter next to the correct answer in the Word Bank.

Word Bank
a. tsar
b. serf
c. patriarch
d. priest
e. liberal
f. boyar

3. What was the title of the head of the Orthodox Church of Russia? __c.__

4. What were the majority of people in Russia in the sixteenth and seventeenth centuries? __b.__

5. What was a Russian noble called? __f.__

6. What was the name for the leader of Russia? __a.__

Learning Coach Guide
Lesson 7: Unit Review

Lesson Objectives

- Demonstrate mastery of important knowledge and skills in this unit.

PREPARE

Approximate lesson time is 60 minutes.

TEACH
Activity 1: Age of Democratic Revolutions (Online)

Instructions

Activity 1. A Look Back (Offline)

History Journal Review

Your student will review what he learned in this unit by going through his History Journal. He should:

- Look at activity sheets and Reading Guides he completed for the unit.
- Review unit keywords.
- Read through any writing assignments he completed during the unit.
- Skim through the chapters in *The Human Odyssey: Our Modern World* that he read in this unit.

Online Unit Review

Your student will go online and review the following:

- Flash Cards: Age of Democratic Revolutions
- Declaring Independence
- Separation of Powers
- French Estates
- Political Spectrum
- Napoleon's Life
- The Revolutionary Americas
- Mapping the Growth of an Empire
- Revolutions Time Line
- Unit 10 Review

Learning Coach Guide
Lesson 8: Unit Assessment

Lesson Objectives

- Recognize major causes, events, and results of the American Revolution.
- Identify major causes, events, and results of independence movements in Latin America.
- Recognize major causes and events of the French Revolution.
- Summarize major ideas and the significance of key documents of the American Revolution and Republic.
- Identify key figures in the Latin American independence movements and their accomplishments.
- Identify Peter the Great, Catherine the Great, and Alexander I and their goals, accomplishments, and failures.
- Identify Napoleon and his primary accomplishments and failures.
- Explain major differences between Russia and western Europe in the seventeenth and eighteenth centuries.
- Summarize the attitude of most colonists toward Britain in 1763 and the reasons for their attitude.
- Summarize the circumstances and events that led to the French Revolution.
- Describe Napoleon's reforms and their significance to the people of France.
- Identify on a map major physical and political features of Europe.
- Describe the social and political structure of Latin American colonies in 1800.
- Identify major physical, political, and cultural features of Latin America.
- Trace significant positions on the political spectrum.
- Identify important physical and political features on maps of Europe and Latin America.
- Identify significant individuals and their contributions to the American Revolution and early republic.

PREPARE

Approximate lesson time is 60 minutes.

Materials

For the Student

🖳 Question Review Table

ASSESS

Unit Assessment: Age of Democratic Revolutions, Part 1 (*Online*)

Students will complete an online test of the objectives covered so far in this unit. The test will be scored by the computer. The attached answer key is the most current and may not coincide with previously printed guides.

Unit Assessment: Age of Democratic Revolutions, Part 2 (*Offline*)

Students will complete an offline Unit Assessment. Print the assessment and have students complete it on their own. Use the answer key to score the assessment, and then enter the results online. The attached answer key is the most current and may not coincide with previously printed guides.

TEACH
Activity 1. Optional: Optional Unit Assessment Review Table (*Online*)

Learning Coach Guide
Lesson 1: Romantic Art in an Age of Revolution

Lesson Objectives

- Recognize that the early nineteenth century revolution in the arts known as Romanticism rejected the ideas of the Enlightenment.
- Describe Romanticism.
- Identify Jean-Jacques Rousseau.
- Identify major writers, artists, and composers of the Romantic period and the kinds of works they are known for.

PREPARE

Approximate lesson time is 60 minutes.

Materials

For the Student

- 🖳 Reading Guide
- 🖳 Romanticism's Other Target
- 🖳 What Makes a Painting "Romantic"?
- The Human Odyssey, Volume 2 edited by Klee, Cribb, and Holdren
- History Journal

For the Adult

- 🖳 Lesson Answer Key

Keywords and Pronunciation

Strum und Drang (shturm oont DRAHNG)

Émile (ay-MEEL)

Eugene Delacroix (del-uh-KWAH)

Franz Joseph Haydn (frahnz YOH-sef HIY-dn)

Horatii (huh-RAY-shee-iy)

Jacques-Louis David (zhahk LOO-ee dah-veed)

Jean-Jacques Rousseau (zhahn-zhahk roo-SOH)

Johann Wolfgang von Goethe (YOH-hahn VOULF-gahng vahn GUR-tuh)

Ludwig van Beethoven (LOOD-vihg vahn BAY-toh-vuhn)

Wolfgang Amadeus Mozart (WOULF-gang ahm-uh-DAY-uhs MOHT-sahrt)

TEACH
Activity 1: Romantic Art in an Age of Revolution *(Offline)*
Instructions

Activity 1. Romantic Art in an Age of Revolution (Offline)

This lesson is designed to be completed in **2** class sessions.

Day 1
Read

Your student will read Chapter 6, from the beginning to "John Constable: Painter of Gentle Landscapes," pages 430–438, and complete **Day 1** of the Reading Guide. When your student is finished, he should use the Lesson Answer Key to check his work, and then place the Reading Guide in his History Journal.

Enlightenment versus Romanticism

Your student will see how Romanticism differed from the earlier thinking of the Enlightenment by completing the Enlightenment versus Romanticism activity.

Let's Get Romantic

Your student will learn how Romanticism affected all areas of artistic endeavor. Today, he'll take a quick look at writers whose words show what it meant to be part of the Romantic movement. He will complete the Romantic Words activity to see the boldness, passion, and "wildness" of these Romantic writers.

Romanticism's Other Target: The Industrial Revolution

Your student will see how Romanticism also reacted against another historical development that was transforming the face of the Western world—the Industrial Revolution. By completing the Satanic Mills sheet your student will learn how one English poet, William Blake, viewed the changes taking place in his country.

Day 2
Read

Your student will read Chapter 6, from "John Constable: Painter of Gentle Landscapes" to the end of the chapter, pages 438–443, and complete **Day 2** of the Reading Guide. When your student has finished, he should use the Lesson Answer Key to check his work, and then place the Reading Guide in his History Journal.

What Makes a Painting "Romantic"?

Your student has seen how Romantic writers expressed themselves. Now he's going to consider how the Romantic movement affected painters by completing the Romantic Painting activity.

ASSESS

Lesson Assessment: Romantic Art in an Age of Revolution, Part 1 *(Online)*

Students will complete an online assessment based on the lesson objectives. The assessment will be scored by the computer. The attached answer key is the most current and may not coincide with previously printed guides.

Lesson Assessment: Romantic Art in an Age of Revolution, Part 2 (*Offline*)

Students will complete this part of the Lesson Assessment offline. Print the test and have students complete it on their own. Use the answer key to score the test, and then enter the results online. The attached answer key is the most current and may not coincide with previously printed guides.

TEACH
Activity 2. Optional: Romantic Art in an Age of Revolution (*Online*)

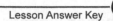

Romantic Art in an Age of Revolution

Day 1

Read

Reading Guide

1. Romanticism was a reaction against the order, harmony, and reason of the <u>Enlightenment</u> period. It represented a revolution in the <u>arts</u>.

2. Instead of emphasizing order, harmony, and reason, Romanticism sought truth in <u>nature or emotion</u>.

3. Name the French philosophe who paved the way for the Romantic movement and name two of his beliefs.
    Rousseau; he believed in the goodness of human nature, the evil of society, that society corrupted, that reason made people cold and unsympathetic toward others, that humans needed freedom.

4. Complete his famous quote: "Man is born free, and <u>everywhere he is in chains</u>."

5. What was the name and nationality of the author of *The Sorrows of Young Werther*? He was a member of the *Sturm und Drang* movement of authors. What does Sturm und Drang mean?
    Goethe, German, Storm and Stress.

6. Name the poet who found inspiration in the natural beauty of the English Lake District.
    Wordsworth.

7. Byron traveled to <u>Greece</u> to help its people fight against the Ottomans. He once declared, "I was born for <u>opposition</u>."

Satanic Mills

1. In the first stanza, how does Blake describe England in that "ancient time" before industrialization?
    Answers may vary. As a time of green mountains and "pleasant pastures," a time when God was present in the land.

2. In the second stanza, into what does the Industrial Revolution turn England?
    Answers may vary. With industrialization, the land filled with mills, and England seemed to undergo a struggle between good and evil, between God and the devil.

3. What image does Blake evoke in the third stanza?
    Answers may vary. Blake prepares for action, like a soldier getting ready for battle.

4. In the fourth stanza, what course of action does he propose?
    Answers may vary. To do all in his power to restore England, to build a new heaven ("Jerusalem") in that once "green and pleasant land."

Day 2

Read

Reading Guide

8. <u>John Constable</u> was a landscape artist who loved to paint the scenery where he grew up, around the River Stour in <u>England or southern England</u>.

9. <u>Eugene Delacroix</u> was a French painter who loved to paint scenes from the exotic places he visited. He also painted *Liberty Leading the People* during the 1830 rebellion.

10. <u>Caspar David Friedrich</u> was a German Romantic artist who painted wild landscapes, such as rocky seacoasts and dark forests.

11. Name the composer who began in the Classical style, became increasingly influenced by Romanticism, and whose music was inspired by the natural world.
    Beethoven.

Explore and Discuss

As you've seen, Romanticism was very much a reaction against the emphasis on reason that was so important to the Enlightenment. It was also a reaction against the Industrial Revolution with its factories and pollution and overcrowded living conditions that, as you'll see in a later lesson, was starting to spread across Europe.

Why might Romanticism have been at odds with such developments?

> **Suggested answer:** In contrast with the mechanization and regimentation of urban life, Romanticism offered freedom and a return to nature. Its stress on the individual and the breaking of rules contrasted with the mass movement and order of factory life. Romantic artists felt alienated from a materialistic society in which machines seemed to be replacing people.

Romantic Art

1. Which historical event does *Liberty Leading the People* depict?
    The 1830 rebellion in Paris.

2. What does it convey about Delacroix's viewpoint or attitude toward the event?
    Delacroix believed different people could come together against tyranny.

3. Who is holding aloft the French flag and what is she doing?
    Liberty holds the flag and she is leading the people.

4. What kinds and classes of people are depicted?
    Young and old, poor and wealthy.

5. Why do you think Delacroix painted himself—the well-dressed man with the top hat—into the scene?
    Answers may vary. To show his sympathy with the cause.

6. What emotions does the painting evoke?
    Answers may vary. Fear, because revolutions are violent; hope, because the people may gain freedom.

Lesson Assessment Answer Key

Romantic Art in an Age of Revolution, Part 2
Answer:

Short-Answer Question

(10 points) What was Romanticism? How did the Romantic arts differ from the arts of the Enlightenment?

> Answers may vary but student should include the following information. Romanticism is a movement in literature and the arts that emphasized an appreciation of nature, feeling, and emotion, and rejected the Enlightenment ideas of reason and intellect. It celebrated the artist as an individual creator. Arts of the Enlightenment focused on certain qualities of Greek and Roman art and literature, such as harmony, order, and balance. They appealed to reason and to the intellect. Romantic arts focused on the appreciation of nature and in the expression of individual emotion.

Award five points if your student correctly defines Romanticism.

Award five points if your student correctly explains how the Romantic arts differ from the arts of the Enlightenment.

Learning Coach Guide
Lesson 2: Britain Begins the Industrial Revolution

Lesson Objectives

- Define Industrial Revolution.
- Identify the factors that allowed the Industrial Revolution to begin first in England.
- Identify Adam Smith and what he is known for.
- Summarize the major ideas of *The Wealth of Nations*.
- Describe the advances made in the textile industry in England in the eighteenth century.
- Describe the beginnings of the coal and iron industries.
- Identify the achievements of individuals who made major contributions to the Industrial Revolution in England.
- Explain the significance of the steam engine to industry.
- Recognize that the changes in manufacturing brought hardships to many people.

PREPARE

Approximate lesson time is 60 minutes.

Materials

For the Student

 📖 In Grandma's Day

 📖 Reading Guide

 📖 The Wealth of Nations

 📖 Why Britain?

 The Human Odyssey, Volume 2 edited by Klee, Cribb, and Holdren

 History Journal

For the Adult

 📖 Lesson Answer Key

TEACH
Activity 1: Britain Begins the Industrial Revolution (Offline)

Instructions

Activity 1. Britain Begins the Industrial Revolution (Offline)

This lesson is designed to be completed in **3** class sessions.

Day 1

Read

Your student will read Chapter 7, from the beginning to "From Handmade to Machine-made," pages 444–451 and complete **Day 1** of the Reading Guide. When your student has finished, he should use the Lesson Answer Key to check his work, and then place the Reading Guide in his History Journal.

A Wealth of Meaning in The Wealth of Nations
Your student will carry out some primary source analysis by completing the Wealth of Nations sheet.
You've Got to Hand It to Mr. Smith!
Your student will see how Adam Smith's capitalist economy can work for the good of all by completing the Invisible Hand activity online.

Day 2
Read
Your student will read Chapter 7, from "From Handmade to Machine-made" to the end of the chapter, pages 451–457, and complete **Day 2** of the Reading Guide. When your student has finished, he should use the Lesson Answer Key to check his work, and then place the Reading Guide in his History Journal.
Why Britain?
Your student will learn about why the Industrial Revolution first began in Great Britain by completing the Why Britain? sheet.
Building a Better Mousetrap
Your student will see how one inventor improves upon the work of his predecessors by completing the Better Mousetrap online activity.

Day 3
"Ah, the Changes I've Seen…"
Your student will see how the Industrial Revolution transformed the lives of the people who lived through it by completing the In Grandma's Day activity.

Activity 2. Optional: Britain Begins the Industrial Revolution (Online)

ASSESS

Lesson Assessment: Britain Begins the Industrial Revolution, Part 1 (Online)
Students will complete an online assessment based on the lesson objectives. The assessment will be scored by the computer. The attached answer key is the most current and may not coincide with previously printed guides.

Lesson Assessment: Britain Begins the Industrial Revolution, Part 2 (Offline)
Students will complete this part of the Lesson Assessment offline. Print the test and have students complete it on their own. Use the answer key to score the test, and then enter the results online. The attached answer key is the most current and may not coincide with previously printed guides.

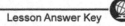

Lesson Answer Key

Britain Begins the Industrial Revolution

Day 1

Read

Reading Guide

1. If *industry* is how things are made, and a *revolution* is an extreme change, then what is an industrial revolution?
   A transformation in how goods are manufactured; an extreme change in the way people work and live; a new way of making products.

2. The Industrial Revolution replaced human and animal power with <u>machine</u> power.

3. During the Industrial Revolution, people moved from the <u>country</u> to <u>cities</u>. In addition, <u>factories</u> replaced <u>homes or houses</u> as the centers of production.

4. In which country did the Industrial Revolution begin?
   Great Britain or England

5. Adam Smith was born in <u>Scotland or Great Britain</u>, he wrote a book called *The Wealth of Nations*, and today is considered to be the father of <u>modern economics or economics</u>.

6. Smith believed that the actions of government often hurt the proper functioning of the economy. Name one such government action.
   The imposition of special taxes, or duties, on imported goods

7. In *The Wealth of Nations,* Smith wrote that markets produced the things that society needed because of the operation of the "<u>invisible</u> hand." This idea forms the basis of a <u>capitalist or market</u> economy.

8. According to Smith, the economy worked best when consumers and producers acted in their own self-<u>interest</u>.

9. Smith also believed that groups of businessmen, known as monopolies, could also hurt the economy. What did he think monopolies would do?
   Fix prices; set prices that were not market prices

A Wealth of Meaning in *The Wealth of Nations*

1. "[Shoemakers] find it for their interest to employ their whole industry in a way in which they have some advantage over their neighbors, and to purchase…whatever else they have occasion for…."
   Translation: Shoemakers should concentrate on what they do best (making shoes) and buy whatever else they need rather than trying to make it too.

2. "Man has almost constant occasion for the help of his brethren, and it is in vain for him to expect it from their benevolence only."
   Translation: People need help from others, but they shouldn't think they'll get that help out of the goodness of people's hearts.

3. "He will be more likely to prevail if he can interest their self-love in his favor, and show them that it is for their own advantage to do for him what he requires of them."
   Translation: He can get people to do what he wants them to do only if he can make it worth their while.

4. "…any man [who] employs capital in the support of industry…neither intends to promote the public interest…He intends only his own gain; and he is in this…led by an invisible hand to promote an end which was no part of his intention."
   Translation: Anyone who invests money in a business is not doing it for anyone else's benefit. He is only doing it for his own benefit. But there are unintended consequences of his actions.

5. "By pursuing his own interest, he frequently promotes that of the society more effectually than when he really intends to promote it."
   Translation: By looking after himself, he often helps everybody else in the society more than he would if he set out with the specific aim of doing just that.

Day 2

Read

Reading Guide

10. In which industry did the Industrial Revolution begin?
    The textile industry

11. John Kay invented the flying shuttle, and James Hargreaves invented the spinning jenny.

12. Richard Arkwright's water frame could make stronger thread than the spinning jenny, and it could make 80 strands at once.

13. Edmund Cartwright invented a mechanical loom powered by a horse or a waterwheel.

14. What important source of power lay beneath England's central and northern hills—a resource important to the development of the iron industry?
    Coal

15. Underground springs often flooded coal mines and had to be pumped out with a crude steam engine known as the Miner's Friend. Name the University of Glasgow student asked to repair one of these broken-down engines in 1763.
    James Watt

16. This Scottish student went on to invent his own, improved piston-driven steam engine that could power all kinds of machines and gave a huge boost to the Industrial Revolution.

17. An English immigrant to the United States named Samuel Slater brought with him extensive knowledge of textile machinery. He built America's first successful cotton mill.

18. Because of steam power, ships no longer had to depend on wind, and mills no longer had to use water for power. Steam-powered machines could work at rates faster than human power ever could.

19. Despite its advantages, the Industrial Revolution also brought many hardships. Name two.
    Long, fourteen-hour workdays; child labor

Short Answer Questions

What was so revolutionary about the Industrial Revolution? In other words, what was the great change that came about because of the Industrial Revolution?

> The Industrial Revolution changed the way people worked because machine power replaced human and animal power.

Which countries did the Industrial Revolution first affect?

> England and other countries in Europe and North America

Even though the Industrial Revolution began in the eighteenth century, not all countries today have undergone an industrial revolution. Why not?

> Because they lack the factors necessary for industrialization such as fuel, a workforce, markets, raw materials, and visionaries and inventors.

Why Britain?

Answer may vary but could include:

> Abundant water power to <u>drive machines</u>
> Textile industry inventions such as <u>the flying shuttle, spinning jenny, mechanical loom, and water frame</u>
> Good harbors and ships for <u>export or free trade or for importing raw materials</u>
> Plentiful supplies of coal for <u>powering Britain's new machines</u>
> Growing city populations for <u>a supply of labor for the factories and mills</u>
> Smith supporters in government who <u>lifted duties to let trade flow freely; encouraged businessmen</u>
> Banks willing to lend money, or capital, in support of <u>new business schemes; businessmen prepared to take risks</u>
> Plentiful supplies of iron ore for the manufacture of <u>tools, parts for looms, jennies, and other machines</u>
> Inventors and thinkers such as <u>Adam Smith, Kay, Hargreaves, Arkwright, Cartwright, and Watt</u>

Day 3

In Grandma's Day

Answer may vary.

Name _____ Date _____

Lesson Assessment Answer Key

Britain Begins the Industrial Revolution, Part 2

Answers:
Short Answer Question

You've now learned about the Invisible Hand and how Adam Smith concluded that people acting in their own self-interest improved things for everybody else. Think of ways in which the Invisible Hand would work in reverse. Describe some ways in which everybody acting in their own self-interest could hurt other people.

> Sample answer: One individual polluting a river by dumping the waste from his factory in it, thereby hurting people who fish in the river. People who refuse to pay taxes for the common good (to provide a police force, national defense, judicial system). Cheats and thieves who steal from others.
>
> Award 3 points (15 points total) for each description.

Learning Coach Guide
Lesson 3. Optional: Your Choice

PREPARE

Approximate lesson time is 60 minutes.

Learning Coach Guide
Lesson 4: A Revolution in Transportation and Communication

Lesson Objectives

- Describe the need for better roads in the 1700s and 1800s and the attempts to improve roads.
- Explain how better transportation led to more trade and lower prices for goods.
- Describe the rise of canal building in the late 1700s and early 1800s.
- Identify Fulton and his contribution to steam-powered boats.
- Identify Stephenson and his contribution to railroad travel.
- Trace the development of railroads in the first half of the nineteenth century.
- Recognize the changes that the revolution in transportation and manufacturing brought.
- Identify Morse and his contribution to rapid communication.

PREPARE

Approximate lesson time is 60 minutes.

Materials

For the Student
- 🖳 A Day in the Life
- 🖳 Reading Guide

The Human Odyssey, Volume 2 edited by Klee, Cribb, and Holdren

History Journal

For the Adult
- 🖳 Lesson Answer Key

TEACH
Activity 1: A Revolution in Transportation and Communication (Offline)
Instructions

Activity 1. A Revolution in Transportation and Communication (Offline)

This lesson is designed to be completed in **3** class sessions.

Day 1
Read

Your student will read Chapter 8, from the beginning to the end of page 467, and complete **Day 1** of the Reading Guide. When your student has finished, he should use the Lesson Answer Key to check his work, and then place the Reading Guide in his History Journal.

When It's Easier by Water

Your student will find out more about a great American canal by completing the Erie Canal activity.

The "Rail Way" to Develop Industry

Your student will learn how the establishment of railroads spurred industrial development by completing the Rail Way activity.

Day 2

Read

Your student will read Chapter 7, from "From Handmade to Machine-made" to the end of the chapter, pages 451–457, and complete **Day 2** of the Reading Guide. When your student has finished, he should use the Lesson Answer Key to check his work, and then place the Reading Guide in his History Journal.

Talking in Code

Your student will find out how to use Morse Code with the help of a website.

A Day in the Life…

Your student will begin to think about all the modern means of transportation and communication he uses in his day-to-day life.

Day 3

A Day in the Life (continued)…

Your student will complete the activity he began the previous day by filling out the Day in the Life sheet.

ASSESS

Lesson Assessment: A Revolution in Transportation and Communication, Part 1 (*Online*)

Students will complete an online assessment based on the lesson objectives. The assessment will be scored by the computer. The attached answer key is the most current and may not coincide with previously printed guides.

Lesson Assessment: A Revolution in Transportation and Communication, Part 2 (*Offline*)

Students will complete this part of the Lesson Assessment offline. Print the test and have students complete it on their own. Use the answer key to score the test, and then enter the results online. The attached answer key is the most current and may not coincide with previously printed guides.

A Revolution in Transportation and Communication

Day 1

Read

Reading Guide

1. Describe the condition of roads in the late 1700s.
   They were muddy and rutted, and made travel difficult and unpleasant.

2. What effect might the condition of roads have on trade? Why?
   It would stunt trade between different locations because it would be too difficult and time-consuming to move goods from one place to another.

3. <u>Turnpikes</u> were roads with gates and guards and could only be used after payment of a toll.

4. Name one advantage of the slightly raised roads built by John McAdam on a foundation of crushed rock.
   They drained well; they held up to heavy traffic.

5. In the early 1800s, improved roads in Britain led to increased trade and lower <u>prices</u>.

6. It has always been easier to move heavy cargo over <u>water</u> than over land. When the need for better transportation became apparent in the late 1700s and early 1800s, there was a surge in the building of <u>canals</u>.

7. Describe the development of canals in Britain.
   Parliament passed laws directing that rivers be dug deeper and wider. Private firms cut canals at key points and connected rivers. Thanks to a web of waterways, boats could reach towns they had never been able to reach before.

8. Canal building also became popular in the United States. Name a famous American canal.
   The Erie Canal

9. <u>Robert Fulton</u> gets popular credit for "inventing the steamboat." He was not only a gifted inventor, but he was also a good <u>businessman</u> who managed to establish a regular steamboat service.

10. In addition to sailing on rivers and lakes, some steamboats even made it across the <u>Atlantic</u> Ocean.

11. Name the inventor of the *Rocket*—the man acknowledged as the "Father of the Railroad."
    George Stephenson

12. As with canal construction, railroad construction also took off in <u>the United States</u>, where some began talking of building a railroad that would stretch all the way from the Atlantic Ocean to the Pacific Ocean.

When It's Easier by Water

1. Which two bodies of water does the Erie Canal link?
   Lake Erie and the Hudson River

2. Why was the canal called "Clinton's big ditch"?
   It was begun by New York Governor DeWitt Clinton, and some skeptics referred to it as his "big ditch."

3. Why did canals have towpaths?
   So people could walk on the bank alongside the canal and horses could tow the barge.

4. What is the purpose of locks?
   Locks allow canals to connect bodies of water of different elevations. Series of locks raise or lower barges throughout the course of a canal.

5. Compare some of the historical and contemporary photographs and images of the Erie Canal. What is the canal most often used for today?
   recreation, sport, leisure activities

The "Rail Way" to Develop Industry

1. British railroads began to link towns that grew into major industrial centers. Why did towns with railroad stations develop quicker than those without them? Why did rail transportation spur industrialization?
   Answers may vary but should include: raw materials could arrive more easily at factories; finished goods could be transported more conveniently to markets; factory and mill laborers could get to work by traveling on the railroads.

2. The building of a railroad was itself a major undertaking, creating jobs for thousands of workers and requiring shipments of various kinds of raw materials and finished products. Name some of the jobs that would be created in a city and the kinds of products and materials that would be required when city leaders decided to build and operate a railroad line.
   Answers should include: construction of a new railroad required the work of engineers, laborers, mechanics, managers, as well as those who provided food and accommodation for these people; steel and coal would be required to build the railroad; food would have to be brought to the city, more stores would be required for selling clothes, household goods, and so on; more homes would have to be built.

3. Today, railroads and locomotives evoke strong emotions in many people, such as nostalgia, sentimentality, and romanticism. This is especially true about steam engines. But nowadays, even though railroads are still important for hauling freight, they carry fewer passengers than in the past. If you have never traveled by train, would you like to? Explain the reasons for your answer. If you *have* traveled by train, describe the experience.
   Answers will vary; some children will have rarely even seen a train, while others may use trains on a fairly regular basis.

Day 2

Read

Reading Guide

13. How did the transportation revolution also lead to a manufacturing revolution?
    Manufacturers now produced goods not just for local consumption, but also for distant consumers and markets. People no longer had to make locally the goods they needed, but could buy them from distant manufacturers instead. Increased demand from growing markets led to an increase in factory size.

14. Samuel Morse invented the electric telegraph, as well as a special code to use on the telegraph, called Morse Code.

15. How did the electric telegraph spread across the United States?
    By following the railroad tracks west

Explore and Discuss

What means of transportation or communication breakthroughs might the future still hold? How would they affect you, the society in general, and our economy?

Answers may vary.

Name _____   Date _____

Lesson Assessment Answer Key

A Revolution in Transportation and Communication, Part 2

Answers:

1. **Possible answer may include:** Goods could move more rapidly from the point of manufacture to the point of consumption. Manufacturers could sell to people all over the country, not just in their own local areas. Manufacturers could produce greater quantities of goods because the market would be bigger. **Award 5 points for each correct example for a total of 10 points.**

2. **Possible answer may include:** Newspapers got information to their readers more quickly. Railroads could keep better track of their trains' locations. Companies, storekeepers, and suppliers could communicate more effectively with each other. Family members who lived far apart could keep in closer contact with each other. Police departments in one town could quickly contact police departments in other towns to help them track down criminals. **Award 5 points for each correct example for a total of 10 points.**

Learning Coach Guide
Lesson 5: Hard Times

Lesson Objectives

- Describe conditions for factory workers in the early nineteenth century.
- Recognize that the workforce included children as young as six and women who were paid less than men.
- Describe living conditions for poor workers in industrial cities.
- Explain the link between lack of sanitation and disease and death rates.
- Identify Charles Dickens and the impact of his writing.
- Identify Queen Victoria.
- Give examples of attempted reforms in industrial cities.
- Identify Karl Marx and what he is known for.
- Summarize the major ideas in Marx's writing.
- Identify Charles Darwin and what he is known for.
- Summarize the major ideas in Darwin's writing.
- Recognize that Thomas Malthus's ideas about population growth influenced politics and literature.

PREPARE

Approximate lesson time is 60 minutes.

Materials

For the Student

- Child Labor
- Oily Business
- Reading Guide

The Human Odyssey, Volume 2 edited by Klee, Cribb, and Holdren

History Journal

For the Adult

- Lesson Answer Key

Keywords and Pronunciation

Das Kapital (dahs kahp-ee-TAHL)

bourgeoisie (bourzh-wah-ZEE) : the middle class

communism : economic system envisioned by Karl Marx in which the government plans the economy and owns most of the land, factories, and other property, and all citizens share in the common wealth

Galápagos (guh-LAH-puh-guhs)

proletariat : factory laborers and others who work for wages

TEACH
Activity 1: Hard Times *(Offline)*
Instructions

Activity 1. Hard Times (Offline)

This lesson is designed to be completed in **3** class sessions.

Day 1
Read

Your student will read Chapter 9, from the beginning to "Karl Marx Criticizes Capitalism," pages 475–483, and complete Day 1 of the Reading Guide. When he has finished, he should use the Lesson Answer Key to check his work, and then place the Reading Guide in his History Journal.

How Hard Was It?

Your student will learn more about the lives of ordinary people, which is an important aspect of the study of history. He will look at some primary sources in the Child Labor activity.

How Hard Are Things Today?

Your student will visit a website to learn about current labor laws in the United States.

What Should Have Been Done?

Your student will consider what, if anything should have been done to improve working conditions, child labor protection, and safety in the workplace. If your student does not have enough time to complete this lesson on **Day 1**, he can begin the **Day 2** lesson by completing this activity.

Day 2
Read

Your student will read Chapter 9, from "Karl Marx Criticizes Capitalism" to "Darwin Sees Competition in Nature," pages 483–486, and complete **Day 2** of the Reading Guide. When he has finished, he should use the Lesson Answer Key to check his work, and then place the Reading Guide in his History Journal.

Communism on the Move

Your student will learn about the rise and fall of communism around the world by completing the Communism on the Move activity.

Day 3
Read

Your student will read Chapter 9, from "Darwin Sees Competition in Nature" to the end, pages 486–489, and complete **Day 3** of the Reading Guide. When he has finished, he should use the Lesson Answer Key to check his work, and then place the Reading Guide in his History Journal.

Theoretically Speaking...

Your student will discuss Darwinism with an adult and understand that not everyone accepts Darwin's ideas.

Mankind's Ongoing Struggle

Your student will examine mankind's ongoing struggle for limited resources by completing the Oily Business activity.

ASSESS

Lesson Assessment: Hard Times, Part 1 (*Online*)

Students will complete an online assessment based on the lesson objectives. The assessment will be scored by the computer. The attached answer key is the most current and may not coincide with previously printed guides.

Lesson Assessment: Hard Times, Part 2 (*Offline*)

Students will complete this part of the Lesson Assessment offline. Print the test and have students complete it on their own. Use the answer key to score the test, and then enter the results online. The attached answer key is the most current and may not coincide with previously printed guides.

Hard Times

Day 1

Read

Reading Guide

1. Describe working conditions for factory workers in the early nineteenth century.
    Factories were dangerous and unhealthy places to work. Workers had to tend their machine for up to sixteen hours a day. They had to observe strict rules and faced punishments for the smallest of breaches.

2. In addition to men, <u>women</u> and <u>children</u> also worked in factories and mills.

3. What was the major difference between the way men and women were paid?
    Women were paid less than men.

4. Working conditions were bad. But for industrial workers, living conditions could be just as bad. Give two examples of such conditions.
    overcrowding, slums, poor sanitation, disease, polluted water, homelessness, inadequate diet

5. <u>Charles Dickens</u> wrote *A Christmas Carol, Oliver Twist, Bleak House,* and *Little Dorrit.* He described an industrial city called Coketown in his 1854 novel, <u>*Hard Times*</u>.

6. In addition to entertaining his readers, what impact did his work have on society?
    His writing helped inform more affluent Britons about the conditions of the poor in industrial cities. It helped create a movement for reform.

7. <u>Queen Victoria</u> ruled England between 1837 and 1901. Name some of the values she emphasized during her reign.
    She emphasized duty, hard work, and proper behavior.

8. Various reformers sought to improve conditions for the industrial poor during the mid-nineteenth century. How did they try to make workplaces safer places to work?
    Reformers introduced new regulations that required erection of fences around dangerous machinery.

9. What efforts were made to improve the lot of overworked workers?
    Reformers passed laws limiting the length of the workday.

10. What development made the streets of London safer?
    the establishment of a new, city-wide police force

11. Which sanitation improvement helped reduce disease in the British capital?
    construction of new sewers that discharged waste farther downstream on the River Thames, away from the city

How Hard Was It?

Child Labor

1. How many abuses can you count in Elizabeth Bentley's testimony? List them all. (You can probably find one for every question asked.)

    She began work at age six. She had to work very long hours—sometimes from five o'clock in the morning until night. She only got 40 minutes during all that time for meals. She was always on her feet. If she got tired or was late, the bosses would strap (or beat) her severely. She didn't have much to eat and what she had was covered with dust.

2. Why might her parents have allowed Elizabeth to perform such work?

    They were probably poor and needed the money. It was considered normal for all poor children to work. Perhaps her father or mother was unable to work and so Elizabeth and her siblings had to help.

3. Why did factory owners hire children like Elizabeth instead of getting adults to do the job?

    They could pay children less. For some tasks, children might not tire so easily as adults. Children would not question orders so much and could be made to do exactly what the owners told them to do.

4. If factory owners and families both wanted child labor to continue, should Parliament still have pressed ahead to reform the system? Why?

    in the interests of the children who had no power to change things; for the greater good of society rather than for the short-term benefit of owners or families; so that children could receive proper education; so that children could have a childhood

Diary

    Answers may vary.

How Hard Are Things Today?

1. What is the minimum age for (nonagricultural) employment?

    The minimum age for employment is fourteen years.

2. How many hours a week may someone of this age work, when school is in session and when it is not?

    Fourteen and fifteen-year-olds may work for a maximum of 3 hours per day and 18 hours per week when school is in session and a maximum of 8 hours per day and 40 hours per week when school is not in session.

3. What is the federal minimum wage?

    The federal minimum wage is $5.15 per hour. However, the minimum wage for youths under 20 years of age is $4.25 an hour.

4. What do you think is the worst teen job and why?

    Answers may vary.

What Should Have Been Done?

    Answers may vary.

Day 2

Read

Reading Guide

12. <u>Karl Marx</u> was a socialist writer who called for the overthrow of capitalism. His major works were *The Communist Manifesto* and *Das Kapital*.

13. He believed that the working class and the middle class struggled against each other for a greater share of <u>economic resources or society's wealth</u>. After a revolution staged by the working class, personal <u>property</u> would no longer exist.

14. What name did he and others use for the working class? What did he call the middle class?
    proletariat; bourgeoisie

Day 3

Read

Reading Guide

15. <u>Charles Darwin</u> was an English scientist who proposed a theory known as "natural selection."

16. The idea that living things have changed over time appeared in the book, *The Origin of Species* in 1859.

17. Thomas Malthus believed that population growth would exceed food supply. How did his beliefs influence society?
    Malthus's beliefs influenced political debates. They were discussed in the press. They were even featured in popular literature, such as in Charles Dickens's *A Christmas Carol*.

Explore and Discuss

Most of us now lead more comfortable lives than the men, women, and children who worked in factories and mills during the nineteenth century. But is it possible that in a hundred years' time, people will look back on the present era and describe it as "hard times"? What could they think was hard about life today?
    Answers may vary.

Did the Industrial Revolution bring positive changes in countries like Great Britain? Give reasons for your answers.
    Answers may vary.

Mankind's Ongoing Struggle

Oily Business

1. What will happen to gasoline prices if demand increases and supplies remain the same or drop?
    Prices will rise.

2. What effect will the cost of gasoline have on the demand for various types of vehicles? What automobiles are likely to sell well? Why?
    Answers will vary but could include: vehicles that use a lot of gas like SUVs may become less popular while hybrids may become more popular.

3. What effect will sales of certain types of cars and trucks have on employment in cities like Detroit where the manufacturing of most large vehicles takes place?
    Factory workers might lose their jobs if sales go down.

4. How might automobile manufacturing in Detroit change?
    Manufacturers might start building other kinds of vehicles that do sell well.

5. How might gasoline prices affect sales of motor scooters?
    sales could increase

6. On a bigger scale, how might the struggle for limited oil resources affect relations between countries?
    Countries that have oil might become more powerful; countries that are powerful but need to import oil might try to take over or control countries that do have oil; there could be wars about oil.

Name _____   Date _____

Lesson Assessment Answer Key

Hard Times, Part 2

Answers:

1. Sample answer: Workers tended machines for up to sixteen hours a day, with just a short break to eat. They had to observe strict rules and had to pay fines if they broke any. Factories were dangerous and unhealthy places to work in.

    Award 5 points (for a total of 15 points) for each of the following references:
    *   hours worked
    *   workplace rules
    *   workplace safety

2. Each correct match is worth 1 point.

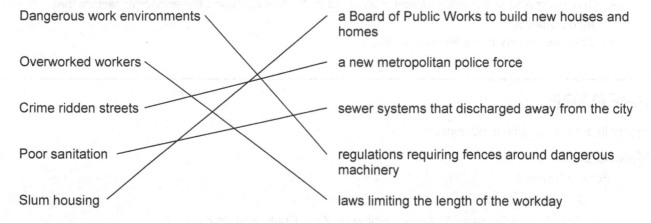

Dangerous work environments — a Board of Public Works to build new houses and homes

Overworked workers — a new metropolitan police force

Crime ridden streets — sewer systems that discharged away from the city

Poor sanitation — regulations requiring fences around dangerous machinery

Slum housing — laws limiting the length of the workday

3. Each correct match is worth 1 point.

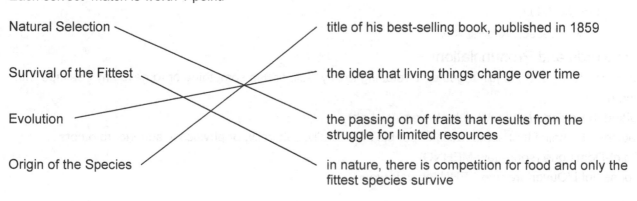

Natural Selection — title of his best-selling book, published in 1859

Survival of the Fittest — the idea that living things change over time

Evolution — the passing on of traits that results from the struggle for limited resources

Origin of the Species — in nature, there is competition for food and only the fittest species survive

---

Learning Coach Guide
Lesson 6: Slavery in the Modern World

Lesson Objectives

- Recognize that Enlightenment ideas about human rights conflicted with the reality of life for most people in the world at the time.
- Describe the slave trade in Africa as it existed by 1700.
- Describe the transatlantic slave trade and its consequences.
- Explain the relationship between slavery and the growth of racism.
- Trace on a map the major routes the slave trade took.
- Recognize that slavery still exists in parts of the world today.
- Compare and contrast the European and Muslim slave trade of Africans with earlier slave systems.
- Identify major leaders of the abolition movement, what they are known for, and the results of their work.
- Summarize the experiences of Equiano.
- Give examples of the kinds of work slaves did in the Americas and the economic factors that encouraged it.
- Describe slavery in the Muslim world.

PREPARE

Approximate lesson time is 60 minutes.

Materials

For the Student

    🖥 Reading Guide

    The Human Odyssey, Volume 2 edited by Klee, Cribb, and Holdren

    History Journal

For the Adult

    🖥 Lesson Answer Key

Keywords and Pronunciation

boycott (BOY-kaht) : to join together in refusing to buy, sell, or use something or to have any dealings with someone

Olaudah Equiano (oh-LOW-duh ek-wee-AHN-oh)

racism : the belief that some races of people are morally, culturally, or physically superior to others

Saint-Domingue (sehn-daw-MEHNG)

Toussaint L'Ouverture (too-SEHN loo-vair-tyour)

TEACH
Activity 1: Slavery in a Changing World *(Offline)*
Instructions
Activity 1. Slavery in a Changing World (Offline)

Day 1
Read

Your student will read Chapter 10, from the beginning to "Slavery and Racism," pages 490–501, and complete **Day 1** of the Reading Guide. When he has finished, he should use the Lesson Answer Key to check his work, and then place the Reading Guide in his History Journal.

Up Close and Personal: Reading a Primary Source

Your student will read again the account by Olaudah Equiano, "Aboard a Slave Ship," on pages 496–497. When he has finished, he should answer the following questions in his History Journal, and then compare his answers to those suggested in the Lesson Answer Key.

1. Why did slavers treat slaves so inhumanely, like squeezing so many of them together in the holds of their ships?
2. How did the slavers try to justify their actions?
3. What explains the slavers' unnecessarily harsh treatment of slaves, like throwing overboard the fish they did not intend to eat rather than giving it to the starving Africans?
4. How might enslaved Africans view not just their slavers but all white people?

Day 2
Read

Your student will read Chapter 10, from "Slavery and Racism" to the end, pages 501–507, and complete **Day 2** of the Reading Guide. When he has finished, he should use the Lesson Answer Key to check his work, and then place the Reading Guide in his History Journal.

Mapping out the Slave Trade

Your student will expand upon what he has learned in the chapter's two maps by completing the African Slave Routes activity.

Day 3
Slavery Time Line

Your student will see how the transatlantic slave trade was not a single event, but a succession of events that saw the trade begin, grow, change, and eventually disappear. He will trace the developments of the slave trade to the New World by completing the Slave Trade Time Line activity.

Abolition Time Line

Your student will see how the Slavery Time Line shows the events surrounding the slave trade, concluding with the abolition of the practice. But a time line oversimplifies events. Your student will find out about some of the key events leading up to Britain's 1833 law to find out just how complicated a process outlawing slavery was.

ASSESS

Lesson Assessment: Slavery in the Modern World, Part 1 (*Online*)

Students will complete an online assessment based on the lesson objectives. The assessment will be scored by the computer. The attached answer key is the most current and may not coincide with previously printed guides.

Lesson Assessment: Slavery in the Modern World, Part 2 (*Offline*)

Students will complete this part of the Lesson Assessment offline. Print the test and have students complete it on their own. Use the answer key to score the test, and then enter the results online. The attached answer key is the most current and may not coincide with previously printed guides.

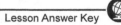

Slavery in a Changing World

Day 1

Read

Reading Guide

1. Did Enlightenment ideas about human rights apply to most people around the world in the eighteenth century?
    No. Such ideas were a far cry from the reality of most people's everyday lives. Three-quarters of the world's population lived in bondage of some sort, as slaves or serfs.

2. For centuries, Africans enslaved other Africans. Name the two later slave trades that transported millions of Africans to distant lands to work.
    the slave trade to the Muslim world and the transatlantic slave trade

3. Slaves marched to the Indian Ocean on Africa's east coast were shipped to <u>Persia or the Arab lands of the Middle East</u>.

4. Slaves marched to the west coast of Africa were shipped across the <u>Atlantic</u> Ocean to the <u>Americas</u>.

5. What killed more than one-third of the slaves before they even reached the coast?
    thirst, disease, and exhaustion

6. Most slaves who were shipped to the Americas worked on <u>sugar</u> plantations.

7. What machine made cotton farming profitable and increased the demand for slaves? Name some of the other kinds of work that slaves performed in the Americas.
    the cotton gin; slaves worked on plantations growing rice, tobacco, and indigo; some worked as household slaves

8. Name the African slave who wrote an account of his experiences in Africa and the Americas and who eventually bought his freedom from his owner, a British naval officer.
    Olaudah Equiano or Equiano

Up Close and Personal: Reading a Primary Source

1. Why did slavers treat slaves so inhumanely, like squeezing so many of them together in the holds of their ships?
    They saw slaves as possessions and slavery as a business. They wanted to maximize the number of slaves aboard each ship to increase the profitability of each transatlantic voyage.

2. How could the slavers try to justify their actions?
    They could claim to be "just doing their job," a job that many others did. They could claim that they were performing a vitally important service—supplying labor to colonies that were in great need of it. They could say they were just trying to feed their own families.

3. What explains the slavers' *unnecessarily* harsh treatment of the slaves, like throwing overboard the fish they did not intend to eat rather than giving it to the starving Africans?
    Perhaps the slavers wanted to demoralize and humiliate the slaves so that they would become unresisting and easier to manage. They wanted to make it clear that they were in total control over every aspect of the slaves' lives. Many viewed Africans as members of an inferior race, not worthy of the dignity and respect accorded other humans.

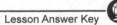

4. How might enslaved Africans view not just their slavers but all white people?
    They may have hated all white people without trying to differentiate between them. Such attitudes may well endure for generations, creating tensions among the races. Another consequence might be widespread belief among whites that blacks were inferior.

Day 2

Read

Reading Guide

9. Why did racism help strengthen the acceptance of slavery?
    It taught that some races, such as the Europeans, were superior to others, such as the Africans.

10. ~~Thomas Clarkson~~ was a young Anglican clergyman who began the abolitionist movement in Britain. He enlisted to the cause a British member of parliament and famous orator named ~~William Wilberforce~~.

11. ~~Elizabeth Cady Stanton~~ was an American abolitionist who also helped organize the world's first conference on women's rights. "We hold these truths to be self-evident: that all ~~men and women~~ are created equal."

12. When did slavery finally come to an end in the Muslim world?
    by the beginning of the twentieth century

Mapping out the Slave Trade

1. Why were so many slaves needed in Brazil and the Caribbean?
    to work on the sugar plantations; a harsh climate, diseases, and terrible living conditions killed many slaves; as slaves died, plantation owners bought new slaves to replace them

2. With relatively few slaves going to North America, why did it end up with so many slaves?
    Many of the slaves were women, and these North American slaves had children, who also became slaves.

3. Why did most slaves in the United States end up in the southern states?
    to work on large agricultural plantations, especially the plantations that thrived with the increased demand for cotton

Lesson Assessment Answer Key

Slavery in the Modern World, Part 2

1. Describe the life and influence of Olaudah Equiano.

   Answers will vary but should include most of the following:

   Equiano was born in Africa and kidnapped into slavery when he was 11 years old. He was captured by slave raiders from a nearby village and sold to a series of African families. Then he was sold to a dealer who supplied slaves to Atlantic coast ships. He endured the horrors of the transatlantic voyage and ended up in Virginia, and was bought by a plantation owner. Eventually, Equiano was bought by a British naval officer who allowed him to buy his freedom. He became a sailor and traveled all over the world. Equiano had learned to read and write English. He wrote a narrative of his life which historians now use to learn more about the lives of slaves.

   Award 2 points for each correct answer for a total of 10 points.

2. Match the slave trade with the description that best suits it. (Award 2 points for each correct match)

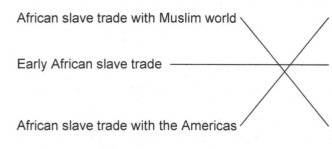

   African slave trade with Muslim world — Slaves were marched to the west coast of Africa, where they were shipped across the Atlantic.

   Early African slave trade — For centuries, Africans enslaved peoples defeated in was and those kidnapped from neighboring villages.

   African slave trade with the Americas — Slave were marched to the Indian Ocean on Africa's east coast, and were shipped to Persia or the Arab lands of the Middle East.

3. Match the abolitionist with his or her description and achievements. (Award 2 points for each correct match)

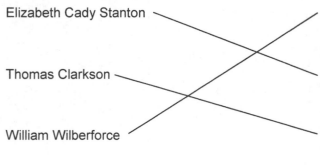

   Elizabeth Cady Stanton — British orator and member of parliament who called for Parliamentary hearing to investigate the slave trade

   Thomas Clarkson — American abolitionist who also helped organize the world's first conference on women's rights, at Seneca Falls, New York

   William Wilberforce — Young Anglican clergyman who began the abolitionist movement in Britain and helped for The Society for Effecting the Abolition of the Slave Trade

Learning Coach Guide
Lesson 7: Unit 11 Review

PREPARE

Approximate lesson time is 60 minutes.

TEACH
Activity 1: Revolutions In Arts, Industries, and Work (Online)

Learning Coach Guide
Lesson 8: Unit Assessment

Your student will take the Unit Assessment for the Revolutions in Arts, Industries, and Work unit.

Lesson Objectives

- Identify Adam Smith and what he is known for.
- Describe the transatlantic slave trade and its consequences.
- Define the Industrial Revolution.
- Explain why the Industrial Revolution began in England in the eighteenth century.
- Describe the Romantic movement in the arts of the early nineteenth century.
- Describe conditions for factory workers in the early nineteenth century.
- Identify major events and individuals of the Industrial Revolution.
- Identify major contributors to the Romantic movement and what they are known for.
- Identify major inventors and inventions of the transportation and communications revolution and the results of their accomplishments.
- Identify Dickens, Marx, and Darwin, and what they are known for.
- Describe living and working conditions for early industrial workers.
- Identify major leaders of the abolitionist movement and what they are known for.

PREPARE

Approximate lesson time is 60 minutes.

Materials

For the Student

⌨ Question Review Table

ASSESS

Unit Assessment: Revolutions In Arts, Industries, and Work, Part 1 (*Online*)

Students will complete an online assessment based on the unit objectives. The assessment will be scored by the computer. The attached answer key is the most current and may not coincide with previously printed guides.

Unit Assessment: Revolutions In Arts, Industries, and Work, Part 2 (*Offline*)

Students will complete this part of the Lesson Assessment offline. Print the test and have students complete it on their own. Use the answer key to score the test, and then enter the results online. The attached answer key is the most current and may not coincide with previously printed guides.

TEACH
Activity 1: Optional Unit Assessment Review Table (*Online*)

Learning Coach Guide
Lesson 1: Picturing Your Thoughts

Lesson Objectives

- Review knowledge gained in the Age of Democratic Revolutions and the Revolutions in Arts, Industries, and Work units.
- Conduct research on examples of progress and hardship in the period from 1700 to 1900.
- Write a thesis statement based on research.
- Support a thesis statement visually.

PREPARE

Approximate lesson time is 60 minutes.

Materials

> For the Student
>> The Human Odyssey, Volume 2 edited by Klee, Cribb, and Holdren

Keywords and Pronunciation

collage : an artwork made by gluing pieces of paper, fabric, photographs, and other objects to a flat surface

inquisitor : one who examines or investigates

juxtaposition : the placing together of two or more contrasting things for the sake of effect

thesis : the focus or main idea of an essay. A thesis states what the essay will prove.

TEACH
Activity 1: Picturing Your Thoughts *(Offline)*
Instructions

Activity 1. Picturing Your Thoughts (Offline)

Day 1
Read, Browse, Peruse

Your student will review the Age of Democratic Revolutions and the Revolutions in Arts, Industries, and Work units, as well as Part 3 of the textbook, pages 348–515. She will prepare for **Day 2** when she will write a thesis statement on the subject of progress and hardship during the period from 1700 to 1900.

Doing the Research

Your student will use online and printed sources to begin research on examples of progress and hardship during the period from 1700 to 1900.

Day 2
Write a Thesis

Your student will write a thesis statement on progress and hardship. A thesis states what the essay will prove.

Re-Research

Your student will continue her research, this time to gather information (visual and statistical as well as written) in support of her thesis.

Day 3
Picture This!
Your student will make a collage supporting her thesis statement with images, quotes, graphs, and other results of her research.

Day 4
Presentation
Your student will finish up her collage and then present it to a member of the family and explain its meaning. She should be ready to answer questions and provide clarifications as needed.

Learning Coach Guide
Lesson 1: Growing Nationalism in Italy and Germany

Lesson Objectives

- Identify the causes of Italian and German unification.
- Identify major events and individuals in the unification of Italy.
- Identify Bismarck and his role in German unification.
- Describe the means Bismarck used to make Germany a unified and powerful nation.
- Define *nationalism*.
- Recognize Napoleon's role in the nationalist movements of the nineteenth century in Europe.
- Recognize the origin of Vatican City as the smallest nation in the world.
- Explain *volksgeist* and its influence on the German peoples.
- Identify the Holy Roman Empire and its situation in the 1800s.
- Locate major German states on a map.

PREPARE

Approximate lesson time is 60 minutes.

Materials

For the Student

- 🖳 Reading Guide
- 🖳 Unified Germany
- 🖳 Unified Italy

    The Human Odyssey, Volume 2 edited by Klee, Cribb, and Holdren

    History Journal

For the Adult

- 🖳 Lesson Answer Key

Keywords and Pronunciation

Reichstag (RIYKS-tahk)

volksgeist (FOLKS-giyst)

Alsace (al-SAS)

Baden (BAH-dn)

chancellor : the title for the head of government in some countries

Count di Cavour (kuh-VUR)

Giuseppe Garibaldi (joo-ZEP-pay gah-ree-BAHL-dee)

Giuseppe Mazzini (joo-ZEP-pay maht-SEE-nee)

Lorraine (luh-RAYN)

nationalism : a strong feeling of attachment to one's own country

prime minister : the leader of a parliamentary government

TEACH
Activity 1: Growing Nationalism in Italy and Germany *(Offline)*
Instructions
Activity 1. Growing Nationalism in Italy and Germany (Offline)

This lesson is designed to be completed in **3** class sessions.

Day 1
Read
Your student will read Chapter 1 from the beginning to "Growing Nationalism in German Lands," pages 522–531, and complete **Day 1** of the Reading Guide. When your student has finished, he should use the Lesson Answer Key to check his work, and then place the Reading Guide in his History Journal.

Italy in 1848 and 1870
Your student will study the map of Italy prior to its unification and then complete the map on the Unified Italy sheet to represent Italy after its unification. He may use the maps on pages 528 and 529 to help him.

Day 2
Read
Your student will read Chapter 1, from "Growing Nationalism in German Lands" to the end, pages 531–537, and complete **Day 2** of the Reading Guide.

Germany in 1848 and 1871
Your student will study the map of Germany prior to its unification and then complete the map on the Unified Germany sheet to represent Germany after its unification. He may use the maps on pages 532 and 536 to help him.

Day 3
Compare and Contrast
Today your student will compare and contrast the means used to unify Italy with those used to unify Germany by completing the Compare and Contrast online activity. He may use his time line, maps, and textbook to help complete this activity.

Major Roles
Some people played major roles in the unification of Germany and Italy. Your student will complete the Major Roles activity. In this activity he will create online Flash Cards describing the roles that some of these major players had in the unification of Germany and Italy.

ASSESS

Lesson Assessment: Growing Nationalism in Italy and Germany, Part 1
(Online)
Students will complete an online assessment based on the lesson objectives. The assessment will be scored by the computer. The attached answer key is the most current and may not coincide with previously printed guides.

Lesson Assessment: Growing Nationalism in Italy and Germany, Part 2
(Offline)

Students will complete this part of the Lesson Assessment offline. Print the test and have students complete it on their own. Use the answer key to score the test, and then enter the results online. The attached answer key is the most current and may not coincide with previously printed guides.

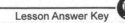

Growing Nationalism in Italy and Germany

Day 1

Read

Reading Guide

1. When did Italy and Germany emerge as independent nations?
   Mid-nineteenth century

2. How did Napoleon play a role in the nineteenth century movements to unify Germany and Italy?
   When Napoleon toppled old governments ruled by dukes and princes, he also spread the ideas of the French Revolution. Napoleon's conquest stirred feelings of nationalism— people began to experience a new sense of unity in their shared dislike of being ruled by foreign kings or emperors. Also, Napoleon brought a sense of unity to people in different states by imposing one currency and by having people from various states fight together in the same army.

3. The strong sense of attachment or belonging to one's own country is called _nationalism._

4. Describe some of the methods young Italian students used to express their support for freedom and unity.
   They staged protests in the streets. They denounced their rulers. They demanded constitutions to protect their rights. They called for a free press. They called for elections so they could choose their own leaders. They wore long hair and sported full beards. Some of the protesters formed secret societies to fight for their causes.

5. Who was Giuseppe Mazzini?
   He was an Italian patriot who formed an organization called Young Italy to unite his fellow countrymen and to free Italy from foreign rule. He believed that people who shared the Italian language, culture, and history should live in a single nation.

6. The Young Italy movement organized uprisings against foreign rule of Italy. Were these uprisings successful? What did the organization persuade many Italians to believe?
   The uprisings were not successful. The rebels were arrested before their revolt even began. Twelve were executed, and a death sentence was put on Mazzini's head. But Young Italy helped persuade many Italians that Italy should be a united country, free of foreign control.

7. Who was Giuseppe Garibaldi? What did he do to earn the title "Hero of Two Worlds"?
   He was an Italian revolutionary who helped unite the Italian peninsula into one nation. He became known as the Hero of Two Worlds because he fought with both Brazilian and Uruguayan revolutionaries and he led campaigns for Italian independence from foreign rule.

8. Garibaldi's troops came to be known as "Redshirts" because their uniforms were red robes that butchers had thrown away.

9. Describe the major events that led to the unification of Italy.
   Answers may vary but should include some of the following events. King Victor Emmanuel appointed Count di Cavour as prime minister of the Kingdom of Sardinia. Cavour arranged a number of secret conversations between the king and Garibaldi. Cavour persuaded the French to help Piedmont if it came under attack from Austria and then he provoked disagreements with Austria that led to war. The French and

Piedmontese fought the Austrians who lost their hold on all the northern Italian states except Venice.

Garibaldi then went to war with the ruler of the Kingdom of the Two Sicilies and won control of all of southern Italy. He turned these lands over to Victor Emmanuel who became king of a united Italy. In 1866, Venice broke away from Austria and joined Italy. Four year later, Victor Emmanuel marched into Rome and declared it the capital of Italy.

10. In 1929, the Roman Catholic Church recognized Italy as a nation with its capital at Rome, and Italy recognized <u>Vatican City</u> as an independent state. Vatican City, a 109-acre territory in the city of Rome, is the world's <u>smallest nation</u>.

Day 2

Read

Reading Guide

11. What was unity like among the German-speaking people in the Holy Roman Empire before and after Napoleon?

Before Napoleon, the German-speaking people in the Holy Roman Empire did not feel a great sense of unity. They shared a language and some customs but did not think of themselves as belonging to one nation. But when Napoleon and his armies invaded, the Germans felt a new sense of unity in their opposition to the French. Many people began to take pride in their German heritage and spirit.

12. Some Germans began to build on an idea proposed by German philosophers. These thinkers wrote that each nation has its own <u>volksgeist</u>, which means the soul of the people.

13. Who was Otto von Bismarck?

He was the Prussian chancellor of the German empire who played a major role in the unification of Germany.

14. What was Bismarck's role in German unification? Describe the methods he used to make Germany a unified and powerful nation.

Answers may vary. He strengthened the Prussian army and built up Prussia's industries. Under Bismarck, Prussia began producing more iron and building more railroads. In 1866, Bismarck purposefully started a quarrel with Austria and war broke out. The Prussian army had a new weapon, the needle gun, which could fire five times a minute, and the Prussian generals used railroads to move their troops rapidly into position. Prussia won the fight, known as the Seven Week War. Prussia became the leading German state, and Bismarck used his new prestige to form a confederation of German states.

Bismarck won the German people over by allowing their leaders to write a constitution and form a parliament. He let all male citizens vote for representatives to the lower house of this new parliament, called the Reichstag. To draw the remaining German states away from Austria, Bismarck instigated a war between Prussia and France. In 1870, Napoleon III declared war on Prussia and nationalist feelings drew the many small German states to Prussia's side. Very quickly, Napoleon III was forced to surrender and the new German Empire now included every German state except Austria. France had to pay Germany five billion gold francs, and turn over Alsace and Lorraine, which were mostly German-speaking provinces rich in coal and iron. The German Empire became one of the most powerful nations in Europe.

Day 3

Major Roles

<u>Giuseppe Mazzini</u>: Answers may vary. He emerged as a powerful voice for freedom and Italian unity. He started an organization called Young Italy. His nationalist goal was to free the Italian states from their foreign rulers and to unify them as an independent republic. His democratic goal was to achieve a freely elected government in a united Italy. Mazzini's work helped persuade many Italians that Italy should be a united country free of foreign control.

<u>Victor Emmanuel II</u>: Answers may vary. He was the ruler of the Kingdom of Sardinia. He was a fiery patriot who wanted to unite Italy under his rule. He made Cavour his prime minister. As king of the united Italy, he marched into Rome and declared it his capital.

<u>Count di Cavour</u>: Answers may vary. He was responsible for getting Emmanuel II and Garibaldi to work together. Prime Minister Cavour schemed to enlist the aid of France against Austria and then he deliberately provoked disagreements with Austria. These disagreements eventually led to war, Austria was defeated and lost control of all the northern Italian states except Venice.

<u>Giuseppe Garibaldi</u>: Answers may vary. Garibaldi was a rebel who wanted a united Italy. Garibaldi and his Redshirts helped the French and the Piedmontese defeat the Austrians. He also seized the Kingdom of the Two Sicilies from the Spanish royal family.

<u>Wilhelm I</u>: Answers may vary. He was the king of Prussia. He appointed Bismarck as his chancellor. He became the Kaiser of a united Germany.

<u>Otto von Bismarck</u>: Answers may vary. Bismarck was the chancellor of Prussia. He strengthened the Prussian army and built up Prussia's industries. He purposefully started a quarrel with Austria, which eventually led to war. He defeated Austria and formed a confederation of German states. He tricked France into declaring war on Prussia. After he defeated the French, he declared the birth of the German Empire, which included every German state except Austria.

Name _____   Date _____

Lesson Assessment Answer Key

Growing Nationalism in Italy and Germany, Part 2

Answers:

1. **Answers may vary but should include at least three of these events**.

   - King Victor Emmanuel appointed the cunning Count di Cavour as prime minister of the Kingdom of Sardinia.
   - Cavour united the king and Garibaldi.
   - Cavour persuaded the French to help Piedmont if it was attacked by Austria and then he provoked disagreements with Austria which led to war.
   - The French and Piedmontese defeated Austria, and all the northern Italian states except Venice joined Piedmont.
   - Garibaldi waged war on the Kingdom of the Two Sicilies and won control of all of southern Italy, which became part of the united Italy.
   - In 1866, Venice broke away from Austria and joined Italy. Four years later, Victor Emmanuel marched into Rome and declared it the capital of Italy.

   Award 4 points (for a total of 12) for each event your student describes correctly.

2. **Answer: Answers may vary but should include at least three of these strategies.**

   - He strengthened the Prussian army and built up Prussia's industries.
   - In 1866, Bismarck purposefully started a quarrel with Austria and war broke out. Prussia became the leading German state, and Bismarck used his new prestige to form a confederation of German states.
   - Bismarck won the German people over by allowing their leaders to write a constitution and form a parliament. He let all male citizens vote for representatives to the lower house of this new parliament, called the Reichstag.
   - To draw the remaining German states away from Austria, Bismarck instigated a war between Prussia and France.
   - Bismarck required France to turn over Alsace and Lorraine, which were mostly German-speaking provinces rich in coal and iron.

   Award 3 points (for a total of 9) for each strategy your student describes correctly.

Learning Coach Guide
Lesson 2: The United States Fights and Unites

Lesson Objectives

- Describe the economic differences between the North and the South.
- Trace on a map the expansion of the United States from 1800 to 1860.
- Recognize that most countries had abolished slavery by the early 1800s.
- Identify Jefferson Davis and Abraham Lincoln and what they are known for.
- Summarize the major events of the Civil War.
- Explain why the Civil War is considered the first modern war.
- Summarize the results of the American Civil War.
- Describe the building of the transcontinental railroad and its significance.

PREPARE

Approximate lesson time is 60 minutes.

Materials

For the Student

🖳 Reading Guide

For the Adult

🖳 Lesson Answer Key

Keywords and Pronunciation

daguerreotype (duh-GEH-roh-tiyp)

Louis Daguerre (lwee dah-gair)

TEACH
Activity 1: Changing Nation (Offline)

Instructions

Activity 1. Changing Nation (Offline)

This lesson is designed to be completed in **3** class sessions.

Day 1

Read

Your student will read Chapter 2 from the beginning to "The First Modern War", pages 538–549, and complete **Day 1** of the Reading Guide. When your student has finished, he should use the Lesson Answer Key to check his work, and then place the Reading Guide in his History Journal.

Changing Nation

During its first hundred years, the United States kept growing until it reached all the way from the Atlantic Ocean to the Pacific Ocean. Your student will go online to review how the country expanded and how it nearly split into two nations.

Day 2

Read

Your student will read Chapter 2, from "The First Modern War" to the end of the chapter, pages 549–557, and complete **Day 2** of the Reading Guide. When your student has finished, he should use the Lesson Answer Key to check his work, and then place the Reading Guide in his History Journal.

The Vital Link

As your student explores the PBS history animation about the transcontinental railroad, he should think about the challenges and obstacles the Central Pacific (CP) and the Union Pacific (UP) railroad companies had to face and how they overcame them. He will be asked to consider which challenges he would include if he were to create a video game or a board game about the race to link the nation and to discuss his choices with an adult.

Guide him to consider the geography of the region as he talks about the game—he may wish to consider how to deal with the Sierra Nevada and the Rocky Mountains, the desert, the Great Plains, the blizzards, and avalanches as well as the difficulty of receiving supplies and feeding and housing thousands of workers in isolated areas of the country.

Day 3

Taking a Stand

The United States was dramatically transformed by the Civil War. Four long years of fighting had killed thousands of people and destroyed homes, crops, factories, and railroads. Despite the terrible devastation, the United States was an enormous country with vast resources and ingenious citizens. During the war many citizens had been forced to abandon their traditional way of life and to learn new skills and roles. The war had settled the question once and for all that the United States should be one, unified nation. But, what kind of nation should it be? In the Gettysburg Address, President Lincoln had presented one vision for the country, but many others had a different idea. Americans faced a bewildering array of decisions about where to live and what to do. What kind of country should they create?

Your student will pretend to be a newspaper editor surveying the state of the nation at the end of the Civil War. He will write an editorial suggesting some steps Americans should take to heal and rebuild the nation.

ASSESS

Lesson Assessment: The United States Fights and Unites, Part 1 (*Online*)

Students will complete an online assessment based on the lesson objectives. The assessment will be scored by the computer. The attached answer key is the most current and may not coincide with previously printed guides.

Lesson Assessment: The United States Fights and Unites, Part 2 (*Offline*)

Students will complete this part of the Lesson Assessment offline. Print the test and have students complete it on their own. Use the answer key to score the test, and then enter the results online. The attached answer key is the most current and may not coincide with previously printed guides.

The United States Fights and Unites

Day 1
Read

Reading Guide

1. In 1803 the United States bought a large chunk of territory from Napoleon; it became known as the Louisiana Purchase. Where was the territory and how did its purchase affect the size of the young nation?
   The Louisiana Purchase extended from the Mississippi River in the east to the Rocky Mountains in the west. It doubled the size of the United States.

2. How did the United States acquire the territory that extends from Texas to California?
   The United States fought a war with Mexico and forced Mexico to give up the territory.

3. The United States grew by leaps and bounds, quickly acquiring territory from Great Britain, France, Spain, and Mexico. Unifying the enormous young nation was a tremendous challenge. What issue threatened to destroy the unity?
   Slavery threatened to divide the large nation.

4. How had Britain and the Latin American nations dealt with the issue of slavery?
   Britain and many Latin American nations had outlawed slavery in the 1810s and 1820s.

5. Compare life in the North and the South by filling in the chart.

	North	South
Type of farming	Small farms	Large plantations
Population	Many European immigrants	Few European immigrants; many black slaves
Cities	Many large cities, including New York, Philadelphia	No very large cities; a few small cities including Charleston, New Orleans
Work force	Farmers, factory workers, businessmen, construction workers (many of them were immigrants)	A few businessmen and plantation owners, many slaves
Attitude toward slavery	Many wanted to abolish slavery	Relied on slaves to plant and pick their crops

6. Many Southerners believed that the federal government could not force its laws onto the states. This idea is called <u>states rights</u>.

7. Label each of the following statements L if it describes Lincoln, D if it describes Davis, and B if it describes both.

   Born in Kentucky __<u>B</u>__

   Grew up as a Southern gentleman __<u>D</u>__

   Taught himself to read and write __<u>L</u>__

   Served four terms in the state legislature __<u>L</u>__

   Served in the United States Senate __<u>D</u>__

   Called slavery a "moral, social, and political evil" __<u>L</u>__

   His greatest loyalty was to his state __<u>D</u>__

   His greatest loyalty was to his country __<u>L</u>__

   Became president of his country __<u>B</u>__

8. How did the southern states react when Lincoln was elected president in 1860?
   Many southern states withdrew from the United States.

9. The Civil War began on April 12, 1861 when Confederate soldiers fired on Fort Sumter in Charleston, South Carolina. Why did the North and the South believe the war would be short?
   Northerners were confident they could quickly win the war because they had more people, more money, and more factories. Southerners thought they could win because they would be fighting on their own territory and because they had many brilliant generals like Robert E. Lee.

10. The Confederates won their first major victory at the Battle of <u>Manassas.</u>

11. Why was the Confederate army so successful during the first two years of the Civil War?
    Lincoln could not find an effective general to lead the Union army. General Robert E. Lee and his Confederate officers were very capable leaders.

12. Why was Great Britain inclined to help the South even though Britain had abolished slavery?
    The South supplied Great Britain with cotton for its textile mills.

13. For Lincoln and the North, the war began as a fight to preserve the <u>Union</u>, but later became a war to end slavery with a document called the <u>Emancipation Proclamation</u>.

14. Why did Lee decide to invade the North?
    Lincoln had imposed a blockade on the southern ports. The South could no longer export its cotton or receive supplies from abroad. Lee realized that a long war would destroy the South if it could not replenish its supplies or get money by selling its crops. Lee took the daring step of invading the North because he hoped he could force Lincoln to end the war sooner.

15. The battle that turned the tide of war in favor of the North was <u>Gettysburg</u>.

16. Who delivered the Gettysburg Address? Why? What vision did it present?

Lincoln delivered the Gettysburg Address to honor the soldiers who had died during the Battle of Gettysburg. In his brief speech, Lincoln presented a powerful vision for the United States as a nation bound together by the idea "that all men are created equal." He went on to say that the United States should have a government "of the people, by the people, and for the people."

17. In what ways was Ulysses S. Grant a very effective military leader?

He believed in striking his enemy hard and moving on. He ordered General Sherman to burn Atlanta and destroy everything in his path as he marched through Georgia and the Carolinas. Grant and his troops captured Petersburg and Richmond, and then trapped Lee near Appomattox, Virginia, and forced him to surrender.

Day 2

Read

Reading Guide

18. How did factories contribute to the Civil War?

Factories supplied uniforms, shoes, bullets, and weapons.

19. How did new weapons affect the war?

The new weapons could be loaded and fired more quickly. The cannons could shoot farther than ever before. The new weapons were deadlier and inflicted much greater damage. Casualties mounted at an alarming rate. At Cold Harbor, Virginia, 8,500 soldiers were killed in eight bloody minutes.

20. What impact did the American Civil War have on the history of Germany?

Otto von Bismarck studied the tactics used in the American Civil War and used them to beat Austria and France. By building railroads and using them to move his troops quickly, Bismarck was able to defeat his foreign enemies and unify Germany.

21. How did news from the battlefields reach the public?

Reporters were able to quickly send news to their newspapers via the telegraph, and for the fist time ever, photographers were able to take pictures of the camps and battlefields.

22. Shortly after the Civil War two new amendments were added to the Constitution. What were they about?

In December 1865, the 13th Amendment was added. It declared that slavery was illegal and all men were born with basic rights, including the right to life and liberty. Five years later the 14th Amendment granted black men the right to vote.

23. In 1865, Americans made slavery illegal. What was the status of slavery in other countries?

Most western European nations had outlawed slavery by 1860. Russia had freed the serfs in 1861, but it took years for the serfs to really achieve true freedom. Most countries in South America had made slavery illegal before 1860, but in Brazil it was legal until the 1880s. In the Muslim world slavery continued through the nineteenth century. In China it became illegal in 1906.

24. How did the Civil War change the role of women?

Women had been actively engaged in the war effort as nurses and hospital volunteers. They had gathered supplies and sewed uniforms. Some had become government clerks or spies. Many northern women had become active in the abolitionist movement. As a result of their contributions, many people believed that women had earned a greater political voice and many women began thinking about greater liberty and rights for women.

25. How did the Civil War affect life in the South?

>The southern way of life had been destroyed. Plantations had been ruined. Landowners had to figure out a new way to farm or rebuild. Four million slaves had been freed and had to face the challenge of building a new way of life. The 11 rebellious states were readmitted to the Union.

26. On May 10, 1869, in Promontory Point, Utah, a rowdy crowd joyously celebrated "the completion of the greatest enterprise ever yet undertaken." How did the construction of the transcontinental railroad change the nation?

>Trains provided a quick, cheap, and easy way of moving goods across the country. The transcontinental railroad linked the entire nation and helped unify it.

27. Who built the transcontinental railroad?

>Two companies built the railroad at the same time. The Union Pacific Company laid the track west from the Missouri River. The Central Pacific Company started in California and worked east. The two companies met at Promontory Point in Utah. Irish, Chinese, Swedish, and German immigrants and slaves did most of the labor.

28. What major obstacles did they face when they were building the railroad?

>They had to overcome major physical barriers such as the Sierra Nevada and Rocky Mountains. They had trouble getting all the supplies they needed to build the tracks, and housing and feeding the workers. They had to fight off attacks from Native Americans.

Thinking Cap Questions

29. Why do many scholars consider the Civil War the first modern war?

>Answers may vary, but should include some of the following facts and ideas.
>The factories and inventions of the Industrial Revolution played a significant role in the Civil War. Factories mass-produced uniforms, supplies, and new lethal weapons that could be loaded and fired quickly. Ironmasters then turned to producing ironclad warships, mines, and a submarine. Communication and transportation improved. Trains moved the troops and their supplies quickly from battlefield to battlefield. The Civil War led to the concept of "total war," in which whole societies were pitted against each other and there was incredible destruction. This new modern warfare led to a staggering death toll. News of the war and troop movements also traveled swiftly on the recently invented telegraph lines. For the first time in history, photography made the public aware of the horrors of war.

30. How did the Civil War transform the nation?

>The South had been devastated and plantations had been destroyed, but the nation had also been strangely renewed by the Civil War. The war established that the United States would be one unified nation and that slavery would be illegal. The nation committed itself to the idea that all men had the right to life and liberty. During the war, factories had geared up to produce war materials. Now the factories turned to producing things to rebuild the nation. Many women had joined the work force during the war, and after the war they began to demand a political voice. Leaders understood the economic and political importance of unifying the nation and they built the transcontinental railroad to link the vast country.

31. After gold was discovered in California in 1849, politicians were eager to build a transcontinental railroad and began to argue about the route. Why did people want the railroad to pass through their region of the country?

>Answers may vary, but should include the idea that railroads could move goods and people much more quickly and easily. As communication and transportation improved, the economy improved.

Name _____   Date _____

Lesson Assessment Answer Key
The United States Fights and Unites, Part 2

Answers:

1. Answers may vary, but should include some of the following ideas.
    The economy of the southern states was based on agriculture. Large plantations in the South grew rice, tobacco, cotton, and indigo. They relied on slave labor to plant and pick the crops. The economy in the northern states was based on small farms and factories. Businessmen were building textile mills and other factories. Cities grew rapidly as people poured in to work in the factories. Railroads and canals were being built to connect the factories with suppliers and customers.

    Award 6 points for stating the economy of the North was based on small farms and industry.
    Award 2 points for each example cited.
    Award 6 points for describing the South as an agricultural or plantation economy based on slave labor.
    Award 2 points for each crop mentioned.

    Total points: 20

2. Answers may vary, but should include some of the following points. Award 5 points for each correct response.
    *   Factories provided mass-produced supplies and equipment.
    *   Modern weapons were more lethal and could be loaded and fired rapidly resulting in many casualties.
    *   Modern railroads allowed troops and supplies to be moved quickly from battlefield to battlefield.
    *   There was "total war", in which entire societies, not just their armies, were pitted against each other.
    *   The telegraph and photography allowed rapid communication.

3. Who does each statement describe? Write **Davis** next to the statements that describe Jefferson Davis and **Lincoln** next to statements that describe Abraham Lincoln.
    Award 1 point for each correct response.

Davis	lived on a southern plantation
Davis	joined the army
Lincoln	lived in the backwoods of Illinois
Davis	became a U.S. senator
Lincoln	taught himself to read and write
Lincoln	joined a debating society
Davis	became the president of the Confederate States of America
Lincoln	became a state legislator
Lincoln	became president of the United States
Davis	his greatest loyalty was to Mississippi
Lincoln	his greatest loyalty was to the Union

Learning Coach Guide
Lesson 3: Age of Innovation

Lesson Objectives

- Explain how steel led to a second industrial revolution.
- Identify Alexander Graham Bell and his accomplishments.
- Identify Thomas Edison and his accomplishments.
- Identify Guglielmo Marconi and his accomplishments.
- Describe advances in fuels in the late 1800s.
- Identify Andrew Carnegie and his accomplishments.
- Describe the evolution of the bicycle into the automobile.

PREPARE

Approximate lesson time is 60 minutes.

Materials

For the Student

📖 Innovators and Innovation

The Human Odyssey, Volume 2 edited by Klee, Cribb, and Holdren

History Journal

For the Adult

📖 Lesson Answer Key

Keywords and Pronunciation

Andrew Carnegie (KAHR-nuh-gee)

Gottlieb Daimler (GAHT-leeb DIYM-lur)

Guglielmo Marconi (gool-YEL-moh mahr-KOH-nee)

Gustave Eiffel (GOUS-tahv IY-fuhl)

Heinrich Hertz (HIYN-rik hurts)

Patent : an official document from the government stating that an inventor owns his or her invention and has the right to make, use, or sell it

TEACH
Activity 1: Innovators and Innovations (Offline)

Instructions

Activity 1. Innovators and Innovations (Offline)

This lesson is designed to be completed in **2** class sessions.

Day 1

Read

Your student will read Chapter 3, from the beginning to "Getting There: From Velocipede to Bicycle" pages 558–565, and complete as much as possible of the Innovators and Innovations sheet.

The Wizard of Menlo Park

When your student has finished reading the textbook and filling out the chart, he will go online and read a short piece of historical fiction about Thomas Edison, The Wizard of Menlo Park. Your student will then write a paragraph explaining why Thomas Edison was such a successful inventor.

Flash Card Maker: Innovators

Your student will go online to create Flash Cards of Henry Bessemer, Andrew Carnegie, Alexander Graham Bell, Thomas Edison, and Samuel Morse.

Day 2

Read

Your student will read Chapter 3, from "Getting There: From Velocipede to Bicycle" to the end of Chapter 3, pages 565–571, and finish the Innovators and Innovations sheet.

When he has finished the sheet, he should use the Lesson Answer Key to check his work.

Spark of Genius: From Hobby Horse to Automobile

Your student will go online and follow the development of one creative idea to the next all the way from hobby horse to automobile.

Activity 2: The Wizard of Menlo Park (Online)

ASSESS

Lesson Assessment: Age of Innovation, Part 1 (Online)

Students will complete an online assessment based on the lesson objectives. The assessment will be scored by the computer. The attached answer key is the most current and may not coincide with previously printed guides.

Lesson Assessment: Age of Innovation, Part 2 (Offline)

Students will complete this part of the Lesson Assessment offline. Print the test and have students complete it on their own. Use the answer key to score the test, and then enter the results online. The attached answer key is the most current and may not coincide with previously printed guides.

Name _____ Date _____

Innovators and Innovations Answer Key

Fill out the chart and answer the questions below.

Innovator	Place	Innovation	Purpose	Impact
Henry Bessemer	England	Special furnace that could turn iron into steel	Produce steel more cheaply	He helped spark a second industrial revolution based on steel.
Charles William Siemens	Germany	Process for making steel in a gas furnace	Produce steel in large quantities	Steel was used to build railroads, tall buildings, and powerful machines.
Andrew Carnegie	Born in Scotland, lived in the United States	Bought iron ore deposits, steel mills, and railroads and ships to transport the materials	Make and sell lots of steel easily	By producing so much steel so efficiently, he helped the United States become an important economic power.
Samuel Morse	United States	Telegraph	Use electricity to send messages over vast distances quickly	By the 1870s there were telegraph offices all across the United States.
Alexander Graham Bell	Born in Scotland, lived in the United States	He and Thomas Watson invented the telephone. Bell and his father-in-law, Gardiner Hubbard started the Bell Telephone Company. His other inventions included a device to remove the outer husk of grains of wheat, methods to record sounds, a method to detect icebergs with echoes, and a method to make water out of vapor.	Communicate quickly over long distances	By the 1890s phone service existed in the United States and Europe.

Innovators and Innovations Answer Key

Innovator	Place	Innovation	Purpose	Impact
Thomas Edison	United States	More than 1,000 inventions, including: Electric voting machine Improved stock ticker "Invention factory"—or research and development lab Lightbulb Electric company Phonograph to record and generate sound One of the first movie cameras	Although Edison is most famous for inventing the lightbulb, he was constantly striving to fix or improve something.	His Invention Factory established the concept of research and development labs, which many corporations use to develop new products. There are electric companies all over the world and people use electricity to light their homes and run their businesses, listen to music, and watch movies.
Jean Lenoir	Belgium	Internal combustion engine	Lenoir wanted to find an alternative to the steam engine that would be more practical, easier to use.	The development of the internal combustion engine meant that engines did not need to be near a constant supply of water, and coal or wood to burn. It led to the development of automobiles and many other machines.
Gottlieb Daimler and Wilhelm Maybach	Germany	Invented the motorcycle by mounting a small, safe internal combustion engine on a bicycle Made a gas-powered, four-wheeled vehicle	Use the internal combustion engine to create more efficient vehicles	The creation of the motorcycle and one of the first automobiles revolutionized transportation and changed society.
Karl Benz	Germany	Made a gas-powered, three-wheeled vehicle with steering wheel and brakes	Use the internal combustion engine to create more efficient vehicles	Some people consider Benz's vehicle the first automobile. The automobile changed society.
Guglielmo Marconi	Born in Italy, lived in England	Wireless telegraph, aerial radio antenna	Send messages anywhere, even to or from moving ships	Messages could be transmitted over very long distances. Other scientists figured out how to send music and voices through radios.

Innovators and Innovations Answer Key

1. How did steel spark a second industrial revolution?

   Iron is strong, but it is hard to shape and can crack relatively easily. Steel is lighter, stronger, and more flexible. When Henry Bessemer and Charles William Siemens figured out ways steel could be produced cheaply in large quantities, they sparked the second industrial revolution. Manufacturers built bigger factories with more powerful machines that could make more goods. Builders could erect taller buildings and railroad workers could build better tracks.

2. People looking for new fuels to run their factories and heat their homes saw promise in petroleum , a liquid mineral found beneath the ground.

3. Why was petroleum superior to coal and wood?

   Petroleum could be processed into gasoline and kerosene, which were easier to transport and burned more easily.

4. Thomas Edison called his research and development lab the " invention factory ."

5. In your opinion, which innovators or innovations contributed most to the industrial development of the late nineteenth century? Make sure you support your answer with ideas, facts, and/or quotations.
   Answers may vary.

Name _____ Date _____

Lesson Assessment Answer Key

Age of Innovation, Part 2

Answers:

1. Answers may vary but should include many of the following facts.
   In 1856 Henry Bessemer invented a special furnace that could cheaply turn iron into steel. A few years later Charles William Siemens pioneered a process for making steel in a gas furnace. The two inventions allowed people to make large quantities of steel relatively cheaply.

   Iron was strong but it was difficult to shape and high winds and heavy loads could crack it. Steel was lighter, stronger, and more flexible.

   With large quantities of relatively cheap steel, industrial nations could build bigger factories with more powerful machines to make more goods than ever before. They could build fine tools with sharp edges. Lightweight steel frameworks made it possible to build very tall buildings. Railroad companies could build better tracks. Steel made the internal combustion engine practical and therefore led to the development of motorcycles and automobiles.

   Total points: 20
   Award 2 points for each innovator.
   Award 2 points for each innovation.
   Award 3 points for explaining why steel was better than iron for construction.
   Award 3 points for each description of how steel changed society.

2. Answers may vary, but should mention how his Invention Factory was the prototype of the research and development labs so many corporations have today and how the development of effective lightbulbs and electric companies transformed society. Edison held the patents for more than 1,000 inventions, including a phonograph and a movie camera.

   Total points: 15
   Award 2 points for each invention.
   Award 3 points for each accurate description of the way the invention affected society.

3. Answers may vary but should include many of the following facts. Jean Lenoir invented the internal combustion engine. Gottlieb Daimler and Wilhelm Maybach invented the motorcycle by mounting an internal combustion engine on a bicycle. Karl Benz invented a gas-powered, three-wheeled vehicle with a steering wheel and brakes. Some people consider it the first automobile. Daimler and Maybach developed a four-wheeled, gas-powered vehicle that other people consider the first automobile.

   Total points: 10
   Award 3 points for each correct example given and 1 point for the logical progression or evolution of the automobile.

Learning Coach Guide
Lesson 4. Optional: Your Choice

PREPARE

Approximate lesson time is 60 minutes.

Learning Coach Guide
Lesson 5: The New Imperialism

Lesson Objectives

- Explain the reasons for the New Imperialism.
- Identify key events and individuals in the expansion of the British Empire.
- Identify on a map the major areas of colonization by Britain, Belgium, Japan, France, Russia, and the United States.
- Describe the way Africa was divided among the European powers.
- Identify major countries and events in the New Imperialism in Asia.
- Describe the effects of colonization on the peoples of the colonized territories.

PREPARE

Approximate lesson time is 60 minutes.

Materials

> For the Student
>> 🖥 Reading Guide
>>
>> The Human Odyssey, Volume 2 edited by Klee, Cribb, and Holdren
>>
>> History Journal
>>
>> 🖥 Dividing Up the Riches
>
> For the Adult
>> 🖥 Lesson Answer Key

Keywords and Pronunciation

Benjamin Disraeli (diz-RAY-lee)

Ferdinand de Lesseps (furd-ee-NAHN duh lay-SEPS)

imperialism : the policy or action by which one country controls another country or territory; it may involve political or economic control

khedive (kuh-DEEV) : the ruler of Egypt

Sa'id Pasha (sah-EED PAH-shah)

TEACH
Activity 1: The New Imperialism (Offline)

Instructions

Activity 1. The New Imperialism (Offline)

This lesson is designed to be completed in **3** class sessions.

Day 1

Read

Your student will read Chapter 4 from the beginning to "King Leopold and the 'Magnificent African Cake,' " pages 572–583, and complete the Reading Guide. When your student has finished, he should use the Lesson Answer Key to check his work, and then place the Reading Guide in his History Journal.

Activity 2: Building the Suez Canal (Online)

Activity 3: Dividing Up the Riches (Offline)

Instructions

Activity 3. Dividing Up the Riches (Offline)

Dividing Up the Riches

After finishing the reading assignment, your student will complete the Africa section of the Dividing Up the Riches sheet to review how Europeans carved up the continent of Africa and tapped its natural resources.

Day 3

Read

Your student will read from "The New Imperialism and the Map of Asia," to the end of the chapter, pages 589–591.

Dividing Up the Riches

Your student will complete the Dividing Up the Riches sheet to review how Europeans and Americans staked claims in Asia and tapped its natural resources. When your student has finished, he should use the Lesson Answer Key to check his work, and then place the Dividing up the Riches sheet in his History Journal.

New Imperialism: Blessing or Curse?

New Imperialism transformed Africa, Asia, and Europe. Your student will pretend to be a newspaper editor writing at the beginning of the twentieth century. Your student will write an editorial about the way New Imperialism has affected the people of Africa and/or Asia.

ASSESS

Lesson Assessment: The New Imperialism, Part 1 (*Online*)

Students will complete an online assessment based on the lesson objectives. The assessment will be scored by the computer. The attached answer key is the most current and may not coincide with previously printed guides.

Lesson Assessment: The New Imperialism, Part 2 (*Offline*)

Students will complete this part of the Lesson Assessment offline. Print the test and have students complete it on their own. Use the answer key to score the test, and then enter the results online. The attached answer key is the most current and may not coincide with previously printed guides.

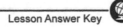

The New Imperialism

Day 1

Read

Reading Guide

1. List four reasons for European interest in overseas colonies at the end of the nineteenth century.
    As Europeans built more and more factories, they searched the rest of the world for raw materials and for markets for the goods their factories produced. European nations were also looking for new supplies of fuel for the large, modern navies they had built. Many Europeans were interested in overseas colonies because they thought they should spread what they considered their superior civilization.

2. The policy of action by which one country controls another country or territory is called imperialism. What does *New Imperialism* refer to?
    New Imperialism refers to the period between the 1870s and 1910 when European nations tried to expand their empires.

3. The British East India Company began to set up trading posts in India in the seventeenth century.

4. During the expansion of the empire, the ruler of England was Queen Victoria.

5. Explain the meaning of the expression, "The sun never sets on the British Empire."
    The empire was so vast that some part of it was always in daylight—it spanned the globe. The empire spread from the Atlantic to the Indian and Pacific Oceans. Its territories included Ireland, Canada, Australia, New Zealand, Ceylon, India, Malaya, Hong Kong, some islands in the West Indies, and large parts of Africa.

6. What triggered the Sepoy Mutiny?
    In 1857, many of the Hindu and Muslim soldiers in India rebelled because they were insulted when they were forced by the East India Company to use greased cartridges made from the fat of hogs and cows. The mutiny released tension that had been building up for years as the British tried to impose their ways on the Indian population. After two years of brutal conflict, the British government shut down the East India Company and starting ruling India directly.

7. Describe the situation in India under British rule.
    The British improved the telephone and telegraph systems and they expanded the network of railroads and irrigation canals, but the vast majority of Indians lived in poverty.

8. Benjamin Disraeli was the British statesman who challenged Britain to become a great, imperial country.

9. Some "social scientists" misused the ideas of Charles Darwin in order to say that some races were superior to others. How did this pseudo-scientific view of race affect the way the British treated their colonies?
    The Office of Colonial Affairs decided that Canada, Australia, and New Zealand could govern themselves to some extent because many of the colonists were of British descent. The Office of Colonial Affairs thought that India, Africa, and other colonies populated by people of different races needed to be controlled more strictly.

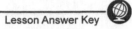

10. <u>David Livingstone</u> was the Scottish missionary, physician, and explorer who shaped the way Europeans thought about Africa.

11. As he traveled throughout Africa, Livingstone tried to convert people to <u>Christianity</u> and tried to help the people find profitable businesses to replace <u>slave trade</u>.

12. Livingstone named the spectacular waterfall he encountered <u>Victoria Falls</u>, to honor the queen of England.

13. When Livingstone returned to Britain he gave many speeches about his experiences in Africa. What were the three main topics of his speeches?
    He talked about the evils of slave trade, the beauty of Africa, and the economic potential of Africa.

14. The Royal Geographic Society persuaded Livingstone to look for the source of the <u>Nile</u>.

15. Why were the French so eager to build a canal across the Isthmus of Suez?
    They wanted to link the Mediterranean and Red Seas so they could avoid a long, dangerous, and expensive journey around Africa to reach their outposts in Asia.

16. Who was Ferdinand de Lesseps?
    He was the Frenchman in charge of building the Suez Canal.

17. How much time did the shortcut between East and West save?
    Before the canal was built, the trip between London and India took about three months. After the Suez Canal was opened, the trip took approximately three weeks.

18. When the Egyptian khedive became desperate for money, he sold his shares in the canal project to <u>Queen Victoria.</u>

19. What relationship developed between Britain and Egypt?
    The British soon dominated Cairo and the rest of Egypt. They had a strong hand in running Egyptian affairs.

Name _____   Date _____

Dividing Up the Riches Answer Key

Africa

1. In 1877, King Leopold of Belgium declared "We must obtain a slice of this *magnifique gateau africain*"—this magnificent African cake. The king was inspired by the writings of <u>David Livingstone</u>. What did his statement mean?

> King Leopold saw a great opportunity for Europeans to spread their civilization and he wanted Belgium to claim some of the raw materials he saw in Africa.

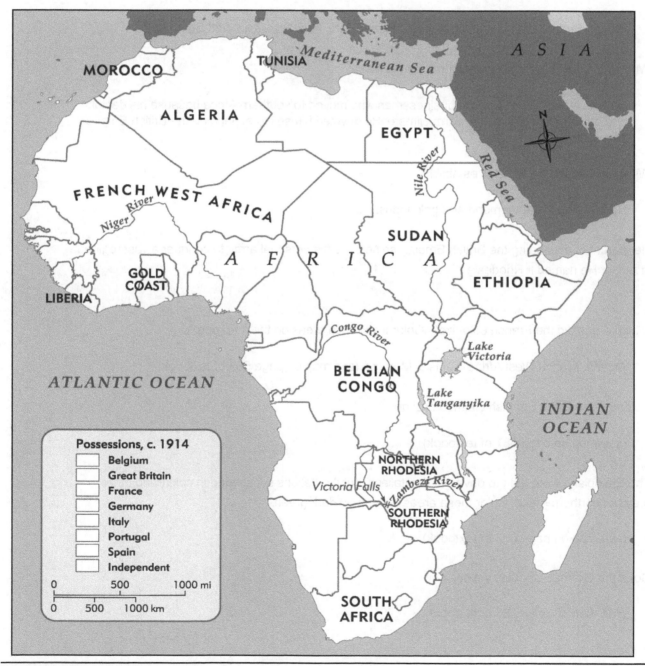

113

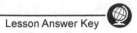

Dividing Up the Riches Answer Key

2. What slice of the African cake did King Leopold claim for Belgium? Color the area on the map pink.

    Congo River basin (see map on page 587 of textbook)

3. What role did the Africans play in the 1884 and 1885 conferences about the future of Africa?

    Africans were not invited to the conferences.

4. Name at least four areas the British claimed. Color the British areas on the map red.

    Egypt, Sudan, Gold Coast, Northern Rhodesia, Southern Rhodesia, and South Africa

5. Who was Cecil Rhodes and what lured him to Africa?

    He was an ambitious English businessman who moved to southern Africa because his doctor had advised him to live in a warm climate. He devoted himself to expanding the British Empire and getting rich.

6. What businesses did Rhodes establish?

    He invested in the diamond and gold industries.

7. He dreamt of expanding the British Empire, so he used his personal army to conquer a vast region in Africa. He named it Rhodesia.

8. Which areas did the French colonize? Color the French areas on the map purple.

    Algeria, French West Africa, Tunisia, Morocco (see map on page 587 of textbook)

9. Color the areas the Spanish claimed orange.

    (see map on page 587 of textbook)

10. The Ethiopians were able to drive out the Italians, but the Italians succeeded in colonizing other areas of northern Africa. Color those areas of the map dark green.

    (see map on page 587 of textbook)

11. Color the German colonies yellow.

    (see map on page 587 of textbook)

Dividing Up the Riches Answer Key

12. Color the areas the Portuguese claimed light green.

   (see map on page 587 of textbook)

13. In all of Africa, only Liberia and   Ethiopia   remained independent.

Color in the boxes on the key with the appropriate colors and compare your map to the one on page 587 of your textbook.

Thinking Cap Question

14. Why were the Europeans able to gain control of nearly the entire African continent?

   Answer may vary but should include most of the following facts. The Europeans had advanced weaponry such as machine guns and repeating rifles. They had railroads and steamships that could be used to move troops and raw materials quickly. They could communicate rapidly by telegraph and telephone.

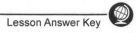

Dividing Up the Riches Answer Key

Asia

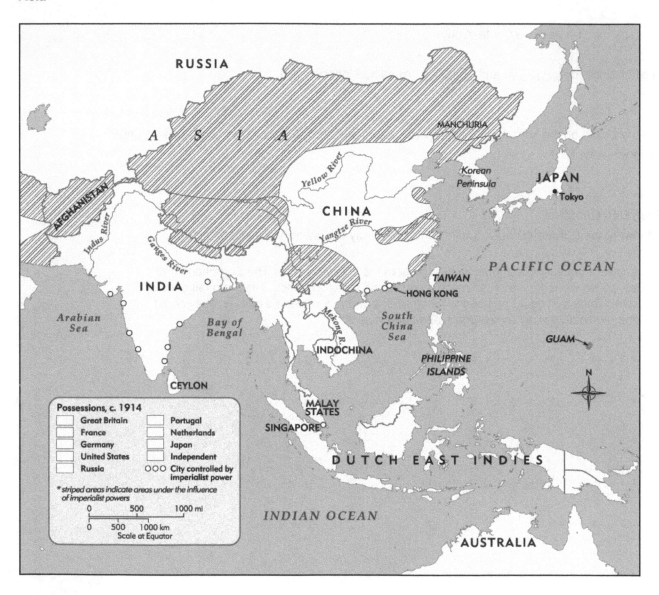

15. What three areas of Asia did the British control in 1914? Color the British areas on the map red.

    India, Ceylon, and the Malay States (Australia looks red on the map on page 589, but is not part of Asia.)

16. List two examples of the New Imperialism in China.

    Britain and other industrial powers demanded trading rights in China. Britain, France, Germany, Russia, the United States, and Japan sent in troops equipped with modern weapons and each claimed a part of China.

Dividing Up the Riches Answer Key

17. The colonizing countries worked out a policy that none of them would close its portion of China to trade with the others. The policy was known as an " open door " policy.

18. Rebels in China tried to end Western domination in the Boxer Rebellion . What happened in the end?

    The industrialized nations crushed the rebellion with their superior weapons and foreigners continued to control China.

19. In 1853 the United States used military power to force Japan to open its door to foreign trade.

20. Color the areas Japan colonized dark green on the map.

    (see map on page 587 of textbook)

21. To avoid conflict, Russia and Britain marked off Afghanistan as a land to separate their empires.

22. In the mid-nineteenth century the French sent troops into Indochina. Which three countries are in the region today? Color the area purple on the map.

    Vietnam, Cambodia, and Laos are in that area today. (see map on page 587 of textbook)

23. The United States gained control of Guam and the Philippine Islands as a result of the Spanish-American War. Color them light green.

    (see map on page 587 of textbook)

Lesson Assessment Answer Key

The New Imperialism, Part 2

Answers:

1. Answers may vary.
   - Award 5 points for describing imperialism as one country controlling another country or territory.
   - Award 5 points for stating that the New Imperialism occurred between 1870 and 1910.
   - Award 5 points for explaining that it was primarily motivated by a need for raw materials, fuel, and markets.

   Total Points _____ (15 points maximum)
   Enter this number online.

Learning Coach Guide
Lesson 6. Optional: Your Choice

PREPARE

Approximate lesson time is 60 minutes.

Learning Coach Guide
Lesson 7: Unit Review

PREPARE

Approximate lesson time is 60 minutes.

TEACH
Activity 1: Nations Unite and Expand *(Online)*

Learning Coach Guide
Lesson 8: Unit Assessment

Lesson Objectives

- Recognize major causes, events, and individuals in the unification of Germany and Italy.
- Define *nationalism* and *imperialism*.
- Identify major contributors to the second industrial revolution and describe their accomplishments.
- Explain the reasons for the New Imperialism of the late nineteenth century.
- Locate on a map major colonial claims in Africa and Asia.
- Describe the effects of colonization on the peoples of the colonized territories.
- Recognize major causes, events, individuals, and results of the American Civil War.
- Describe the second industrial revolution.

PREPARE

Approximate lesson time is 60 minutes.

Materials

For the Student

💻 Question Review Table

ASSESS

Unit Assessment: Nations Unite and Expand, Part 1 (*Online*)

Students will complete an online assessment based on the lesson objectives. The assessment will be scored by the computer. The attached answer key is the most current and may not coincide with previously printed guides.

Unit Assessment: Nations Unite and Expand, Part 2 (*Offline*)

Students will complete this part of the Lesson Assessment offline. Print the test and have students complete it on their own. Use the answer key to score the test, and then enter the results online. The attached answer key is the most current and may not coincide with previously printed guides.

TEACH
Activity 1: Optional Unit Assessment Review Table (*Online*)

Learning Coach Guide
Lesson 1: Organizing for Change

Lesson Objectives

- Describe the conditions city dwellers faced in places such as Paris, London, and New York.
- Explain the role of trade unions and describe the methods they used to improve working conditions.
- Identify significant leaders of the women's rights movement of the late nineteenth and early twentieth centuries and describe their methods and accomplishments.
- Explain the reasons for the population growth in cities of the 1800s.
- Identify Louis Pasteur and describe his accomplishments.
- Describe the conditions most industrial workers faced.
- Give examples of the ways Paris and New York addressed their problems.
- Review historical events.

PREPARE

Approximate lesson time is 60 minutes.

Materials

For the Student

📖 Reading Guide

The Human Odyssey, Volume 2 edited by Klee, Cribb, and Holdren

History Journal

For the Adult

📖 Lesson Answer Key

TEACH
Activity 1: City Life (Offline)
Instructions

Activity 1. City Life (Offline)

Day 1
Read

Your student will read Chapter 5 from the beginning to "Louis Pasteur: Fighting Disease," pages 592–600, and complete **Day 1** of the Reading Guide. When your student has finished, she should use the Lesson Answer Key to check her work and then place the Reading Guide in her History Journal.

New York, New York

When she has finished the reading activity, your student will calculate the population density of New York City and go back online to get an impression of what life was like in the bustling city by completing the New York, New York activity and visiting a website.

Day 2
Read

Your student will read Chapter 5, from "Louis Pasteur: Fighting Disease" to the end of the chapter, pages 600–609, and complete **Day 2** of the Reading Guide.

Triangle Shirtwaist Fire

To learn more about the working conditions immigrants faced in the late nineteenth century, your student will go back online and click The Triangle Shirtwaist Fire. Then she will answer some questions in her History Journal.

Women on the March

To review some of the important steps women took to obtain equal rights, your student should complete the Women on the March activity online.

Day 3

Your student will pretend to be an immigrant at the beginning of the twentieth century and create a scrapbook showing life in the big city. She should be sure to highlight some of the recent improvements and to discuss some of the problems that still exist. She may need to do additional research from the websites listed in Resources to create her scrapbook.

Lesson Resources

ASSESS

Lesson Assessment: Organizing for Change, Part 1 (*Online*)

Students will complete an online assessment based on the lesson objectives. The assessment will be scored by the computer. The attached answer key is the most current and may not coincide with previously printed guides.

Lesson Assessment: Organizing for Change, Part 2 (*Offline*)

Students will complete this part of the Lesson Assessment offline. Print the test and have students complete it on their own. Use the answer key to score the test, and then enter the results online. The attached answer key is the most current and may not coincide with previously printed guides.

TEACH
Activity 2: Organizing for Change (*Online*)

Organizing for Change

Day 1

Reading Guide

Read

1. In the nineteenth century urban population grew dramatically. Why did so many people move to the cities?

    Many people moved to the cities to find jobs in the factories.

2. What were the working conditions like in most factories?

    People worked very long hours in noisy, dark, and crowded factories and earned very low wages.

3. What was Paris like when Napoleon III became emperor in 1852?

    The narrow, winding streets were dark and filled with horse manure and garbage. The city was riddled with crime and diseases. Newcomers were pouring into the crowded city and squeezing into rat-infested housing.

4. How did Napoleon III and Eugène Haussmann transform Paris?

    Haussmann tore down slums and eliminated the narrow streets in large sections of the city. He installed new aqueducts, sewers, an underground rail system, and elegant gas lights. He built impressive government buildings, more than 273,000 new dwellings, broad new tree-lined boulevards, parks, monuments, and traffic circles.

5. Describe New York City and its population in 1900.

    In 1900, New York had the world's busiest ports, busiest banks, and busiest industries. The rapidly growing population had reached three million; 80 percent of the residents were European immigrants.

6. Why did New York face a special challenge trying to handle its growing population?

    The heart of the city is on the small island of Manhattan and until steel was mass-produced and elevators were invented, it was not possible to build buildings taller than four or five stories.

7. Who created Central Park and how did it differ from most European parks?

    Frederick Law Olmsted wanted the enormous park to be a place of calm and harmony that seemed entirely natural unlike the formal parks in most European cities. Central Park included many wide open areas and almost five million trees and shrubs.

New York, New York
Population density

1870	57,720 per square mile
1880	53,306 per square mile
1890	42,746 per square mile
1900	41,780 per square mile
1910	30,690 per square mile

Population density of New York City today: 25,545
Population density of Cheyenne, Wyoming today: 2,611
Reactions and answers may vary.

Day 2

Read

8. How did Louis Pasteur establish his reputation?
> Louis Pasteur had made his reputation by studying how tiny microbes affected wine. He proved that heat could kill the microbes that had been spoiling the wine. The process he developed to keep wine, milk, and other food products from spoiling became known as *pasteurization*.

9. What happened when Pasteur injected an old culture of chicken cholera microbes into a hen? What happened when he injected a fresh culture of chicken cholera microbes into the hens that had been injected with the old culture?
> The hen injected with old culture only became mildly sick and recovered quickly. When the hens were reinjected with fresh culture, they were not affected.

10. Pasteur also created vaccines against <u>anthrax</u> and <u>rabies</u>.

11. Ironworkers, coal miners, and other workers began to organize trade unions. What did trade unions do?
> Unions bargained with employers for better hours, improved wages, and better working conditions.

12. When collective bargaining failed, employees sometimes went on <u>strike</u>.

13. Why did the workers at the Bryant & May match factory in England go on strike?
> The workers—mainly women—objected to fines and rules against talking, dropping matches, or visiting the restroom without permission. When some employees were fired for protesting against the rules, all the workers went on strike. The owners finally gave in and rehired the protestors and eliminated the fines.

14. Employers created blacklists of union organizers. People on the lists were frequently <u>fired</u> or denied <u>employment</u>.

15. A British immigrant named <u>Samuel Gompers</u> organized the American Federation of Labor. By 1900, it had more than a million members.

16. In 1848 women held the first conference for <u>women's rights</u> in Seneca Falls, New York.

17. Who was arrested for trying to cast a vote in the U.S. presidential election in 1872? Why?
> Susan B. Anthony was arrested and fined because women were not allowed to vote.

18. Why did many people object to giving women the right to vote?
> Some people said women were not intelligent enough to vote. Others thought that giving women the right to vote might destroy the family.

19. Who was Emmeline Goulden Pankhurst? Why did she become famous?
> Emmeline Pankhurst campaigned in Britain for the right of women to vote and she founded the Women's Social and Political Union, or WSPU. She and other WSPU members interrupted political meetings and once tried to storm the House of Commons in Parliament to demand the right to vote. She was jailed repeatedly and went on hunger strikes until all British women were finally allowed to vote in 1928.

20. Which nation became the first to grant women full voting rights?
> New Zealand

Triangle Shirtwaist Fire

1. How did workers and trade unions draw attention to poor working conditions?
   They held demonstrations, wrote flyers and newspaper articles, and went
   on strike.

2. Did most people in the nineteenth century support the business owner or the workers and the unions?
   Most people were suspicious of the unions and supported the business owners.

3. How did the public react to the Triangle Shirtwaist Fire?
   Many members of the public were outraged. Newspapers published political cartoons and critical articles and editorials condemning the terrible working conditions and demanding that the government make and enforce workplace safety laws.

4. Who held more power in the nineteenth century—the workers or the factory owners?
   Was the balance of power changing in the early twentieth century?
   During most of the nineteenth century people were sympathetic to factory owners and were suspicious of labor unions. However, as people became more aware of the terrible working conditions in some of the factories, workers and unions gradually gained support. In the early twentieth century, unions gained political power, laws were passed, and gradually factory conditions began to improve.

Day 3

Answers may vary.

Lesson Assessment Answer Key

Organizing for Change, Part 2

1. Explain what women had to do to earn the right to vote. Why was voting considered controversial? Who led the fight for women's suffrage? What methods did they use?

   Answers may vary, but should include most of the following facts. In the nineteenth century many people said women were not intelligent enough to vote. Others thought that giving women the right to vote might destroy the family. But many women were determined to vote and to be treated equally.

   In 1848 women gathered in Seneca Falls, New York and established an agenda for the women's rights movement. Women such as Susan B. Anthony worked hard to earn the vote. They spoke out, organized meetings and demonstrations, and risked being sent to jail by voting when it was not legal for women to vote. In Britain suffragists such as Emmeline Goulden Pankhurst and her daughters fought desperately for the right to vote. Emmeline founded the Women's Social and Political Union, or WSPU. She and other WSPU members interrupted political meetings and once they tried to storm the House of Commons in Parliament to demand the right to vote. When Parliament did not respond to their demands, the women turned to more violent methods. Emmeline Pankhurst was jailed repeatedly and went on hunger strikes until all British women were granted voting rights in 1928.

   Total points: 15

   Award 5 points for accurately explaining why voting was controversial.
   Award 5 points for accurately identifying Susan B. Anthony and describing the methods American suffragists used to earn the right to vote.
   Award 5 points for accurately identifying Emmeline Pankhurst and describing the methods British suffragists used to obtain voting rights.

   or

    What working conditions did most factory workers face in the nineteenth century? What did trade unions do to improve the working conditions? How did the owners respond?

   Answers may vary, but should include many of the following facts. People worked very long hours in noisy, dark, and crowded factories and earned very low wages. People organized trade unions to demand better wages, better and safer working conditions, and better hours. The unions tried to use collective bargaining to negotiate improvements. If the negotiations failed, the workers went on strike.

   Many owners agreed to some of the workers' demands because they did not want their businesses to have to shut down. However, some employers blacklisted employees and others locked them out.

   Total points: 15

   Award 5 points for accurately describing work conditions.
   Award 5 points for accurately describing the actions of trade unions.
   Award 5 points for accurately describing the owners' response to labor's demands.

2. Louis Pasteur
3. heat

Learning Coach Guide
Lesson 2: Reaching Millions

Lesson Objectives

- Explain the meaning of the term *mass society*.
- Explain why new leisure activities became popular in the late 1800s, and give examples of those activities.
- Identify William Randolph Hearst and Joseph Pulitzer and what they are known for.
- Summarize the methods Henry Ford used to bring automobiles to the masses.
- Identify new technologies that contributed to mass entertainment.
- Explain the role of universal education in the economic progress of Western Europe and the United States.
- Describe the changes that occured in sales and marketing and the reasons for them.

PREPARE

Approximate lesson time is 60 minutes.

Materials

For the Student

📖 Reading Guide

The Human Odyssey, Volume 2 edited by Klee, Cribb, and Holdren

History Journal

For the Adult

📖 Lesson Answer Key

Keywords and Pronunciation

Aristide Boucicaut (ah-ree-steed BOO-sih-koh)

Baron Pierre de Coubertin (koo-behr-tan)

Bon Marché (bohn mar-SHAY)

mass production : the production of goods in large quantities

mass society : large numbers of people

middle class : the social class of people who are neither rich nor poor, which includes most skilled workers

vaudeville (VAWD-vil)

TEACH
Activity 1: Turn of the Century (Offline)

Instructions

Activity 1. Turn of the Century (Offline)

This lesson is designed to be completed in **3** class sessions.

Day 1

Turn of the Century

Your student will begin the lesson online by seeing how much she knows about the popular innovations of the late nineteenth and early twentieth century.

Read

Your student will read Chapter 6 from the beginning to "Mass Publishing: Pulp Fiction and Yellow Journalism," pages 610–619, and complete **Day 1** of the Reading Guide. When your student has finished, she should use the Lesson Answer Key to check her work, and then place the Reading Guide in her History Journal.

Day 2

Read

Your student will read Chapter 6, from "Mass Publishing: Pulp Fiction and Yellow Journalism," to the end of the chapter, pages 619–625, and complete **Day 2** of the Reading Guide.

What Happened?

Your student will write a brief paragraph or create a diagram to show how some inventions affected society.

Day 3

Ford's Revolution

Your student will write a document-based essay describing how Henry Ford revolutionized the auto industry and the lives of workers all around the world. Your student will base the essay on what she knows about the time period and Henry Ford, and on the documents found at the Henry Ford websites listed below. She must include quotations from Henry Ford and others who were involved in the company in her essay.

ASSESS

Lesson Assessment: Reaching Millions, Part 1 (*Online*)

Students will complete an online assessment based on the lesson objectives. The assessment will be scored by the computer. The attached answer key is the most current and may not coincide with previously printed guides.

Lesson Assessment: Reaching Millions, Part 2 (*Offline*)

Students will complete this part of the Lesson Assessment offline. Print the test and have students complete it on their own. Use the answer key to score the test, and then enter the results online. The attached answer key is the most current and may not coincide with previously printed guides.

Reaching Millions

Day 1

Reading Guide

Read

1. How had life in Western Europe changed between 1800 and 1900?
   Most Europeans in 1800 were poor peasants trying to scratch out a living from the soil. By 1900 there were bustling cities with lights, trolley cars, telephones, factories, and a growing middle class.

2. What is the middle class?
   The middle class is the group of people who are neither rich nor poor. Many people in the middle class work in offices, stores, factories, and other businesses.

3. What is "mass society"?
   The word *mass* refers to a large quantity or amount. By 1900 there was a substantial middle class, and factories were mass producing goods. A growing number of people were looking for ways to amuse themselves, which led to mass entertainment such as movies, amusement parks, travel, and spectator sports. Methods of communicating such as telephones and telegraph were referred to as mass communication.

4. How did stores change in the nineteenth century?
   Aristide Boucicaut and his wife built the first department store. It was an enormous store that displayed the merchandise in different departments, which customers could browse through. (In the past customers had not been able to see merchandise; they had just asked the sales clerk for the items they wanted.) The Boucicauts also established fixed prices in their department store; previously customers had bargained with the sales clerks. The Boucicauts kept the prices low because they bought large quantities of merchandise. The Boucicauts allowed people to buy merchandise on credit, which was unusual at that time.

5. How did marketing to people in rural areas change during the nineteenth century?
   Modern machinery helped the farmers earn extra income so they had money to spend. Traveling salesmen charged high prices and offered farmers little variety. Richard Warren Sears decided to send people in rural areas catalogs that offered goods for sale so they could shop by mail. By the end of the century, Sears and his partner, Alvah Curtis Roebuck were mailing out catalogs that had more than 500 pages and offered thousands of products. Soon many other companies started selling products through catalogs.

6. As shorter work hours and labor-saving home appliances began to allow people some leisure time, people started to seek new forms of entertainment. Many headed toward "trolley parks," which offered <u>dance halls</u>, <u>picnic tables</u>, and <u>carnival rides</u>.

132

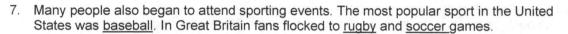
7. Many people also began to attend sporting events. The most popular sport in the United States was <u>baseball</u>. In Great Britain fans flocked to <u>rugby</u> and <u>soccer</u> games.

8. In the United States of the 1890s vaudeville became very popular. What was it?
   Vaudeville shows were variety shows that featured a wide variety of short acts that included everything from animal acts to short plays, and comedians or jugglers.

9. Technology also contributed to new forms of entertainment. After Thomas Edison invented the <u>phonograph</u>, people began to listen to famous singers in their own homes.

10. Thomas Edison also invented the Kinetoscope. What was it and how did it affect entertainment?
    It was the earliest device to show "moving pictures" or movies. The movies were very short and jerky. At first, the brief movies just showed actions such as a sneeze, a boxing match, or a dance. Gradually movies got longer and they began to tell a story. In 1894 the first Kinetoscope parlor opened. Eventually they began projecting the moving pictures onto a large screen. The first movie theaters were called nickelodeons. Most of the early movies were silent. Nickelodeons declined as larger movie theaters were built to show longer movies.

Day 2

Reading Guide

Read

11. Why did people in the second half of the nineteenth century have more and more books to read?
    High-speed printing presses led to mass printing and "dime novels" or "penny dreadfuls" became very popular.

12. What were *pulps*?
    They were magazines printed on cheap wood-pulp paper. They usually included science fiction and tales about cowboys in the American West.

13. The two publishers who transformed the daily newspaper into a form of entertainment were <u>Joseph Pulitzer</u> and <u>William Randolph Hearst</u>. Their newspapers included many sensational stories, sports, comics, and news about entertainment.

    When did European nations begin offering education to all children? When did the United States start public education?
       It was not until 1870 that the British Parliament passed a law saying all children should be educated and until the 1890s that the public schools were really funded. Germany advanced public education in the 1870s and 1880s. In the United States, Massachusetts passed a law requiring children to attend school in the 1850s and by 1890 most American children were attending school.

14. How did education affect the economic status of most nations?
In countries that had universal public education most of the adults could read so the countries developed an economic edge over countries that did not educate all their children.

15. When Henry Ford was growing up, what did he like to do in his spare time?
He loved to take things apart and figure out how they worked.

16. Henry Ford became obsessed with building a quadricycle. What was it?
It was a small chassis with four bicycle wheels and a simple gasoline engine. Ford also called it his "gasoline buggy."

17. What was Ford's primary goal when he started the Ford Motor Company?
He wanted to build a motor car for the masses.

18. Ford finally figured out a way to build his Model T cheaply enough so that middle class people could afford it. How did he do that?
He reorganized his factory into an assembly line of workers. Conveyor belts would deliver the automobile parts to the workers. Each worker would perform a specific task or add a specific part before the conveyor belt moved the automobile along to the next worker.

19. How did the car change America?
Highways were paved, people began to work, shop, and go to school farther away from their homes. Suburbs and shopping malls flourished.

What Happened?

Phonograph: When Thomas Edison invented the phonograph in 1877 he brought music out of the concert hall, and, eventually, into the home. His first recordings were on cylinders covered with tin foil. Emile Berliner developed flat discs, which could be mass produced and made better recordings. Eldridge Johnson designed a better phonograph with a new kind of motor. Berliner and Johnson developed affordable phonographs called Victrolas. "Pop stars" emerged as radio and records became so popular.

Kinetoscope: Thomas Edison's moving pictures on a Kinetoscope eventually led to the development of an enormous movie and entertainment industry. At first people could only watch a few flickering images that showed brief movements. In 1894, a Kinetoscope parlor opened where customers could view five different Kinetoscopes. A few years later one of Edison's employees made an eight-minute movie that actually told a story. Movies became much more popular when people began to project the movies onto a large screen. Movie theaters, called Nickelodeons, opened all across the country. At first they showed silent films. Gradually businessmen built larger theaters and producers made longer films with sound. Today millions of people watch movies everyday in theaters—and on television and DVDs in their homes.

High-speed press: The invention of the high-speed press revolutionized the publishing industry and turned reading into a popular form of mass entertainment. In the early days, "dime novels," "penny dreadfuls," sensational newspapers, and pulp magazines attracted many readers. As more and more people received an education, more and more books, newspapers, and magazines are produced all over the world.

Day 3

Ford's Revolution

Answers may vary. Your essay should mention assembly-line production of automobiles, a guaranteed salary of five dollars a day, and a five-day workweek. Your answer may also mention paved highways, gasoline stations, suburbs, shopping malls, travel, drive-ins, long-distance commutes and other consequences of the popularity of cars.

Sources:
"Henry Ford: Why I Favor Five Days' Work With Six Days' Pay"
Primary source: interview on website
Published in October 1926
General audience
Samuel Crowther

"Henry Ford's Revolution for the Worker"
Secondary source: website article at www.AmericanHeritage.com
Posted January 5, 2006
General audience
Christine Gibson (former *American Heritage* editor)

Lesson Assessment Answer Key

Reaching Millions, Part 2

1. Briefly describe mass society and explain how it affected the economy and leisure activities.

   Answers may vary. By 1900 the middle class had grown considerably. The word mass refers to a large quantity or amount. Members of the growing middle class began to have some leisure time and looked for ways to amuse themselves, which led to mass entertainment such as movies, amusement parks, travel, and spectator sports. Factories began mass production of goods. Department stores were built and mass merchandising through catalogs became very popular. People began communicating with instruments of mass communication such as telephones and telegraph.

   Total points: 15

   Award 5 points for describing mass society.

   Award 5 points for describing how mass society affected the economy.

   Award 5 points for describing how mass society affected leisure activities.

Learning Coach Guide
Lesson 3: Culture Shocks

Lesson Objectives

- Recognize that while many people saw the nineteenth century as a time of great progress, others questioned materialism and human nature.
- Identify Freud and describe his accomplishments.
- Explain the goals and techniques of the Impressionist, Postimpressionist, Cubist, and abstract painters.
- Identify examples of Impressionist, Postimpressionist, Cubist, and abstract art and artists.
- Recognize the goals and characteristics of modernism in music.
- Identify Zola and describe his Naturalist beliefs.

PREPARE

Approximate lesson time is 60 minutes.

Materials

For the Student

🖳 Reading Guide

The Human Odyssey, Volume 2 edited by Klee, Cribb, and Holdren

History Journal

For the Adult

🖳 Lesson Answer Key

Keywords and Pronunciation

L' Assommoir (lah-sohm-wahr)

Ballets Russes (ba-lay roos)

Claude Monet (klohd moh-NAY)

Coupeau (coo-poh)

Cubism : a 20th-century style of art developed by Pablo Picasso and Georges Braque in which the artist reduces an object to its basic geometric shapes and shows it from a number of different angles at the same time

Edgar Degas (ed-gahr duh-GAH) : a French Impressionist artist

Edouard Manet (ay-DWAR ma-NAY)

Georges Braque (zhorzh brahk)

Gervaise (jehr-vehz)

Giverny (zhee-vehr-NEE)

Igor Stravinsky (EE-gor struh-VIN-skee)

Impressionism : an artistic movement in which painters gave an "impression" of a scene rather than trying to make their painting depict reality with photographic accuracy; major Impressionists include Degas, Manet, Monet, Renoir, and Cassatt

Jan Vermeer (yahn vur-MAYR)

Mary Cassatt (kuh-SAT)

Pierre Auguste Renoir (pyehr aw-GOOST ruhn-wahr)

Sigmund Freud (froyd)

Vincent van Gogh (van GOH) : Dutch Post-Impressionist artist

Wassily Kandinsky (VAH-si-lee kan-DIN-skee)

Émile Zola (ay-meel ZOH-luh)

TEACH
Activity 1: 1889 World's Fair *(Offline)*

Instructions

This lesson is designed to be completed in **3** class sessions.

Day 1
1889 World's Fair

To review the progress that had occurred during the nineteenth century and to focus on the prosperity that many people were beginning to enjoy, your student will create a list of items she would have showcased if she had been in charge of the 1889 World's Fair (the *Exposition Universelle*).

Read

Your student will read Chapter 7 from the beginning to "New Artistic Visions: Impressionism and After" pages 626–633, and complete **Day 1** of the Reading Guide. When your student has finished, she should use the Lesson Answer Key to check her work, and then place the Reading Guide in her History Journal.

Day 2
Read

Your student will read Chapter 7, from "New Artistic Visions: Impressionism and After" to the end of the chapter, pages 633–639, and complete **Day 2** of the Reading Guide.

Artistic Styles

Your student will go back online to review Impressionist, Postimpressionist, Cubist, and abstract art in the Artistic Styles activity.

The Rite of Spring

Your student will go online to listen to a brief excerpt from Igor Stravinsky's *The Rite of Spring*. Then she will write a paragraph in her History Journal describing the music and her reaction to it.

Day 3
Interview

Your student will choose one writer, composer, or artist from the chapter and do more research about that person's life and work. Then your student will "conduct an interview" with that person by writing a series of questions and answers based on the research. Your student may wish to consult Grolier's online encyclopedia or the following websites ith the Resources section.

ASSESS

Lesson Assessment: Culture Shocks, Part 1 (*Online*)

Students will complete an online assessment based on the lesson objectives. The assessment will be scored by the computer. The attached answer key is the most current and may not coincide with previously printed guides.

Lesson Assessment: Culture Shocks, Part 2 (*Offline*)

Students will complete this part of the Lesson Assessment offline. Print the test and have students complete it on their own. Use the answer key to score the test, and then enter the results online. The attached answer key is the most current and may not coincide with previously printed guides.

Culture Shocks

Day 1

Reading Guide

Read

1. When the French hosted the World's Fair in 1889, what were they celebrating? What were they trying to showcase?

   The French were celebrating the one hundredth anniversary of the French Revolution. They were showcasing the progress that had taken place since the Revolution.

2. Why were the late 1800s and the early 1900s known as the *"Belle Epoque"*?

   "Belle Epoque" means *"Beautiful Time."* Europe was powerful, prosperous, and at peace. It was enjoying all the advances in science, technology, education, and human rights that had occurred during the Scientific Revolution and the Industrial Revolution.

3. Despite the signs of prosperity, some people expressed doubts. Who were they and why were they concerned?

   Philosophers, psychologists, and novelists wrote about an irrational and dark side of human nature. Artists questioned long-held assumptions about the relationship of art to reality. Some people wondered whether material progress really made people happier or life any more meaningful.

4. According to most people in the nineteenth century, what caused mental illness?

   Most people did not know what caused mental illness. Some speculated that it was caused by injury to the body or brain. Others thought that emotionally painful events caused it.

5. Who was Sigmund Freud? What did he think caused mental illness?

   Freud was a physician who lived in Vienna, Austria. He believed that mental illness was caused by conflict between the conscious and the unconscious parts of the mind. We think and solve problems with our conscious mind. The unconscious is filled with powerful instincts and desires. Freud thought we were driven by powerful, irrational forces from the unconscious. Freud thought the struggle to repress those forces led to mental illness.

6. What is *psychoanalysis*?

   It is a process developed by Freud to understand the patient's unconscious desires. One way to unlock the unconscious mind is to analyze dreams.

7. What did the Naturalists believe?

> The Naturalists were influenced by the ideas of Charles Darwin. They believed that human beings were shaped by their environment. Naturalist novelists depicted human life with the same objectivity that scientists used to observe nature.

8. Who was Émile Zola?

> He was a French novelist and one of the greatest Naturalists.

9. Write a short paragraph describing Zola's purpose in writing *L'Assommoir*. Do you think he succeeded in doing what he set out to do?

> *L'Assommoir* tells the story of a young woman who works in a laundry. She marries a young worker who gets injured. Zola describes how poverty and life in the slum destroy the couple. Zola's Naturalist novel shows how poor people living in slums are crushed by the hopelessness of their surroundings. Opinions about his success may vary.

Day 2

Reading Guide

Read

10. How did photography complicate the question of artistic truth?

> Artists began to wonder how they could compete with true-to-life photography. Many people who wanted a family portrait or a picture of a landscape began turning to photographers rather than to painters.

11. What did the Impressionists think art should convey? How did they convey it?

> Impressionists tried to show the changing effects of light, such as the shifting colors of the evening air or water. They created an impression of a fleeting moment of reality by using short brushstrokes and vivid dabs of color.

12. Name some of the famous Impressionist painters.

> Edgar Degas, Edouard Manet, Pierre-Auguste Renoir, Claude Monet, and Mary Cassatt were major Impressionist artists.

13. Vincent van Gogh admired the Impressionists, but he had one criticism. What was his criticism?

> He thought their method did not allow the artist to really express his emotions.

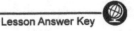

14. Fill out the chart below.

Style	Famous Artists	Goals	Techniques
Impressionist	Edgar Degas Edouard Manet Claude Monet Pierre-Auguste Renoir Mary Cassatt	Emphasize light and color to capture an impression or fleeting moment of reality.	Short brushstrokes, vivid color
Postimpressionist	Vincent van Gogh	Continue to depict light, and use bright colors and short brushstrokes, but emphasize emotions. Artists' styles varied.	Expressive colors and brushstrokes
Cubist	Pablo Picasso Georges Braque	Break down and imaginatively reassemble objects. (Thought art did not have to copy textures, colors, and shapes of real objects.)	Eliminate the illusion of space, use geometric shapes, show subject from several angles.
Abstract	Wassily Kandinsky	Create art out of the elements of art itself, such as line, color, shapes, light, and texture.	Banish identifiable objects from artwork. Stress color, shapes, and light.

15. The composer most associated with the beginning of modern music is Igor Stravinsky. His ballet, *The Rite of Spring*, shocked the music world when it premiered in 1913.

16. How did modern music differ from traditional music?
    The instruments seemed to struggle with each other instead of harmonizing. The music did not have a melody or a predictable rhythm—it was composed of harsh and dissonant sounds.

Artistic Styles

1. The Impressionists used short, visible brushstrokes.

2. The Impressionists tended to use brighter, sunnier hues. They frequently painted outdoors and tried to reproduce the effect of light on their subject.

3. Van Gogh used thick, bold brushstrokes and vibrant colors. Most people think the bright yellows and oranges create a joyful feeling in this painting.

4. Picasso has included many bold, jagged lines. He has included triangles, ovals, and polygons. This painting looks very flat, but it shows the weeping woman's face from the front and side (profile) simultaneously.

5. Kandinsky has included many colors in this painting. There are many shades of gray, red, blue, yellow, cream, and white. Kandinsky has included many fine lines. Some of them are straight, some are wobbly, some are jagged, and many of them are curved. Most of the shapes are free-flowing and there are few well-defined ones.

6. Postimpression. The painting has many of the visible brushstrokes, obvious patches of paint, and some of the bright colors that Impressionists used, but the painting shows very strong emotion.

7. This is an abstract painting. It does not have a recognizable subject. It shows lines and blobs in various colors.

8. This is a Cubist painting. It is relatively flat, it includes many geometric shapes, and shows various parts of the violin from different angles.

9. This is an Impressionist painting. You can see many short brushstrokes in a variety of colors. The artist has captured an "impression" or fleeting moment of the ballet. The artist shows the audience in the dark and shows that the spotlight is on the ballerina in yellow.

Lesson Assessment Answer Key

Culture Shocks, Part 2

1. At the end of nineteenth century, many people appeared confident and prosperous, but others had doubts. Write a paragraph describing the two points of view. Explain who was likely to hold each point of view and why.

   Answers may vary, but should include most of the following information.
   People looked around and saw many new factories making new products. They saw growing cities, tall skyscrapers, and people with time to enjoy themselves. The prosperity gave them confidence. But some philosophers, psychologists, novelists, and artists sensed that people had doubts and anxieties. The psychologists and artists began to explore the irrational side of human nature, and in the process revolutionized our understanding of the human mind and our concepts of art and music.

   Total points: 20
   Award 10 points for describing entrepreneurs, industrialists, and the majority of the population as feeling confident in response to the prosperity they saw.
   Award 10 points for stating that philosophers, psychologists, writers, and artists began to explore the irrational and dark side of human nature and it altered the way they created art and music.

Learning Coach Guide
Lesson 4: Remarkable Individuals

Lesson Objectives

- Identify key individuals who shaped the modern era and describe their contributions to society.

PREPARE

Approximate lesson time is 60 minutes.

Materials

For the Student

🖥 Reporter's Checklist

For the Adult

🖥 Reporter's Checklist Answer Key

TEACH
Activity 1: The Modern World *(Offline)*

Instructions

This lesson is designed to be completed in **2** class sessions.

Day 1

Your student will go online to create a special edition of a newspaper called *The Modern World.* She will research and briefly describe the contributions of remarkable leaders in several fields.

Day 2

Your student will choose the most influential person of the era and write an article explaining her choice. The article should describe the person and his or her work, and why she chose that person as the most influential person of the era.

Then your student will create a cartoon or caricature of "the modern man" or "the modern woman." The cartoon should show—perhaps humorously—some of the activities, customs, or fashions people enjoyed in 1900.

Lesson Assessment

There is no assessment in this lesson.

Name _____   Date _____

Reporter's Checklist

Who	Where	What (Contributions to Society)
Aristide Boucicaut	Paris, France	Created the first department store and introduced new marketing ideas
Thomas Edison	United States	Many inventions including lightbulbs, phonographs, Kinetoscope, and early moving pictures
Sigmund Freud	Vienna, Austria	Founder of psychoanalysis who theorized that the mind is divided into conscious and unconscious parts
Frederick Law Olmsted	United States	Designed New York City's Central Park and many other parks in other cities
Emmeline Pankhurst	England	Fought for women's suffrage and founded the Women's Social and Political Union
Louis Pasteur	France	Proved that microorganisms cause disease; developed process of pasteurization and the first vaccines for rabies and anthrax
Pablo Picasso	Spain	One of the most influential of all modern artists, he and Georges Braque were the first to create Cubist art
Joseph Pulitzer	United States	Transformed the daily newspaper into a form of entertainment
Richard Warren Sears	United States	Started mail-order business with catalogs
Igor Stravinsky	Russia	Composer most associated with the beginning of modern music; composed *The Rite of Spring*

Learning Coach Guide
Lesson 5. Optional: Your Choice

PREPARE

Approximate lesson time is 60 minutes.

Learning Coach Guide
Lesson 6: Unit Review

PREPARE

Approximate lesson time is 60 minutes.

TEACH
Activity 1: Answers and Questions *(Online)*
Instructions
History Journal Review

Your student will review what she learned in this unit by going through her History Journal. She should:

- Look at activity sheets and Reading Guides she completed for the unit.
- Review unit keywords.
- Read through any writing assignments she completed during the unit.
- Review any offline assessments she took during the unit.
- Skim through the chapters in *The Human Odyssey: Our Modern World* that she read in this unit.

Online Unit Review

Your student will go online and review the following:

- New York, New York
- Triangle Shirtwaist Factory
- Women on the March
- Turn of the Century
- Artistic Styles
- The Modern World
- Modernistic Trends
- Groundbreakers
- Inventions and Nationalism Time Line

Learning Coach Guide
Lesson 7: Unit Assessment

Lesson Objectives

- Recognize changes in the way many people lived as a mass society developed.
- Identify major leaders of the labor and women's movements and their methods for achieving reform.
- Describe the goals and techniques of painters, authors, and composers.
- Describe living and working conditions in the cities of the 1800s and how they were improved.
- Identify major innovators in the new mass society and what they are known for.

PREPARE

Approximate lesson time is 60 minutes.

Materials

For the Student

🖳 Question Review Table

ASSESS

Unit Assessment: Answers and Questions, Part 1 (*Online*)

Students will complete an online assessment based on the unit objectives. The assessment will be scored by the computer. The attached answer key is the most current and may not coincide with previously printed guides.

Lesson Assessment: Answers and Questions, Part 2 (*Offline*)

Students will complete this part of the Lesson Assessment offline. Print the test and have students complete it on their own. Use the answer key to score the test, and then enter the results online. The attached answer key is the most current and may not coincide with previously printed guides.

TEACH
Activity 1: Optional Unit Assessment Review Table (*Online*)

Learning Coach Guide
Lesson 1: Rising Expectations in Waning Empires

Lesson Objectives

- Explain the reasons for discontent in old empires in the late nineteenth and early twentieth centuries.
- Recognize the Serbs as an example of ethnic groups whose nationalism led to independence movements within the Ottoman Empire.
- Identify Franz Josef and the methods he used in trying to maintain his empire.
- Analyze excerpts of Gandhi's philosophy of nonviolent resistance.
- Identify Sun Yat-sen and his role in Chinese independence.
- Recognize changes to the maps of empires in the late nineteenth and early twentieth centuries.
- Summarize Gandhi's development as a champion of Indian independence from Britain.
- Describe the role of nationalism in changing imperialism in the early twentieth century.
- Recognize the city of Vienna and the cultural attractions it offers.

PREPARE

Approximate lesson time is 60 minutes.

Materials

For the Student

- Cataloging the Past
- Reading Guide
- The Human Odyssey, Volume 2 edited by Klee, Cribb, and Holdren
- History Journal

For the Adult

- Lesson Answer Key

Keywords and Pronunciation

Antonin Dvorák (AHN-toh-neen DVOHR-zhahk)
Antonín Dvorák (AHN-toh-neen DVOHR-zhawk)
Croats (CROH-ats)
Czechs (cheks)
Shanghai (shang-HIY)
Slovaks (SLOH-vahks)
Slovenes (SLOH-veens)
Sun Yat-sen (soun yaht-sen)

TEACH

Activity 1: Rising Expectations in Waning Empires *(Offline)*

Instructions

Day 1

Read

Your student will read Chapter 8, from the beginning to "India's Mohandas Gandhi," pages 640–647, and complete **Day 1** of the Reading Guide.

Putting the Habsburgs on the Map

Your student will go online and review the Habsburg Map activity to see what time did to the great empire of the Habsburgs.

Cataloging the Past

Your student will begin a chart that examines some of the ethnic groups, nationalists, and revolutionaries we've met in the chapter. He will start the Cataloging the Past activity.

Day 2

Read

Your student will read Chapter 8, from "India's Mohandas Gandhi," to the end pages 647–653, and complete **Day 2** of the Reading Guide. When he has finished, he should use the Lesson Answer Key to check his work, and then place the Reading Guide in his History Journal.

Finding India and China on the Map

Before proceeding further, your student will make sure he can locate India and China on a map.

Document Analysis: Getting to Know Gandhi

Your student will go online and analyze Gandhi through his words by completing the Gandhi's Quotations activity.

Day 3

In Tribute…

Your student will go back to his by-now-completed Cataloging the Past chart and select one of the leaders or peoples whose accomplishments he finds most noteworthy, impressive, and compelling. He should write a tribute to that leader or those peoples giving emphasis to the methods used to accomplish their goals. To prepare for the tribute, he will carry out research online as required.

ASSESS

Lesson Assessment: Rising Expectations in Waning Empires, Part 1 (*Online*)

Students will complete an online assessment based on the lesson objectives. The assessment will be scored by the computer. The attached answer key is the most current and may not coincide with previously printed guides.

Lesson Assessment: Rising Expectations in Waning Empires, Part 2 (*Offline*)

Students will complete this part of the Lesson Assessment offline. Print the test and have students complete it on their own. Use the answer key to score the test, and then enter the results online. The attached answer key is the most current and may not coincide with previously printed guides.

TEACH
Activity 2. Optional: Rising Expectations in Waning Empires (*Online*)
Instructions
Your student will pay a virtual visit to the Habsburg's imperial capital by visiting the Vienna Tourist Information website.

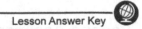

Rising Expectations in Waning Empires

Reading Guide

Day 1

Read

1. In the late nineteenth and early twentieth centuries, the new force of nationalism began to motivate many subject peoples living in old empires. Nationalists did not feel allegiance to their imperial masters. Instead, they felt a sense of belonging and loyalty to their own <u>country, nation, culture, traditions</u>.

2. What did nationalists seek instead of imperial rule?
    self-rule, freedom, independence

3. One of the old empires was the Ottoman Empire. Name three of the four regions of that empire.
    Southeastern Europe, Asia Minor, North Africa, Middle East

4. In 1683, the Ottomans had advanced to the very gates of Vienna before they were <u>defeated, turned back</u> by the Austrians. Since that time, slowly but surely, the Ottoman Empire began to <u>shrink</u> and various subject peoples struggled for their <u>independence, freedom</u>.

5. In southeastern Europe, the Ottoman Empire faced a particularly stiff challenge from nationalists. Name the ethnic group that fought for and won its independence from imperial rule in 1878.
    the Serbs

6. You've read how Ottoman troops advanced to the very gates of Vienna in 1683. Since that time, the empire seemed to be in retreat. What territory did the Ottomans lose next?
    Hungary

7. By 1812, the Ottomans had lost two large chunks of land in the north and east. What bodies of water do they border?
    the Black Sea and the Caspian Sea

8. More territories had slipped from Ottoman control by 1878. Name two European nations that had emerged as independent countries. (You learned about one of them in the chapter. You read about the other nation in an earlier chapter—and about the English poet Lord Byron's attempt to help liberate it from Ottoman rule.)
    Serbia and Greece

9. What happened to Serbia and Greece? What is their status today?
    They maintained their identities and are still independent countries. Serbia more or less occupies the same territory as that liberated from the Ottomans in 1878; Greece has expanded beyond the territory liberated from the Ottomans.

10. The Ottoman Empire was in decline, known to the other great powers of the day as "the Sick Man of Europe." In fact, most of its remaining territory was not in Europe but in North Africa and the Middle East. Name two modern-day countries in each of those regions.
    Egypt, Libya, Tunisia; Iraq, Syria, Lebanon, Israel (per the textbook maps, Egypt can be considered as part either of North Africa or of the Middle East)

11. Ultimately, the Ottoman Empire shrunk to Asia Minor, with only a small toehold in Europe. What is the name of the country occupying that part of the world today?
    Turkey

12. <u>Franz Josef</u> ascended the imperial Habsburg throne in 1848. Immediately, he had to put down a revolt against his rule in <u>Hungary</u>.

13. Later, however, he maintained Habsburg power in his far-flung empire by compromising with his Hungarian subjects. How did he do this?
    He granted them their own parliament and constitution. Or, he created the Dual Monarchy.

14. He was less successful in winning over the Czechs, Slovaks, Croats, and Slovenes of his empire. What were these people collectively known as?
    Slavs, Slavic people

15. With which ethnic group would the Habsburgs have particular trouble that would plunge the nations into a world war?
    the Serbs, Serbia

Day 2

Read

16. Who was the champion of India's independence movement from Britain?
    Mohandas Gandhi, Gandhi

17. He was raised in India as a traditional <u>Hindu</u>, but was educated as a lawyer in <u>England</u>, where he adopted many Western ways.

18. In which country did he first practice as a lawyer and work for the rights of the Indian people?
    South Africa

19. Name the "weapon" that he used to "fight" against injustice and oppression.
    nonviolence or passive resistance

20. Who is known as "The Father of the Chinese Revolution"?
    Sun Yat-sen

21. Name two things that angered this revolutionary leader.
    The presence (and dominance) of foreigners in China; the treaty ports; the weakness of China's Manchu rulers

22. In 1911, he became the first <u>president of the new Chinese republic</u>.

23. All across the globe, nationalism challenged the power of imperialism in the early twentieth century. Nationalists from <u>Serbia</u> won their freedom from the Ottomans in 1878. The Habsburgs had to concede some self-rule to the <u>Hungarians</u>. The nonviolent resistance of Gandhi threatened Britain's hold on <u>India</u>. And Chinese nationalists drove Western imperialists out of the <u>treaty ports</u> on the coast.

Explore and Discuss
Is imperial rule always a negative experience? Are there positive things about empires? The Roman Empire, for example, brought law and order and roads and aqueducts to Gaul. But what if the people still don't want to be ruled by a foreign power? What if some, half, or most of the people *do* want foreign rule and the benefits it brings? Is there such a thing as a good empire? Give examples to back up your answers.

Lesson Assessment Answer Key

Rising Expectations in Waning Empires, Part 2
Answers:

1. (10 points) Mohandas Gandhi led India to independence from Britain and is one of the world's great historical figures. Summarize how he developed during the three major stages of his life, and lived in three different countries.

Answer should include points like these: Gandhi was raised a traditional Hindu but left his home in India to study law in London. In England, he adopted Western styles and manners. Later, as a lawyer in South Africa, he struggled for the rights of Indians living there and against the discrimination they suffered at the hands of white people. Returning to India, he took up the cause of Indian independence—his homeland's freedom from British rule.

2. *(10 points)* According to Gandhi, "nonviolence [is] a weapon." Who could use this weapon? What did he believe it could achieve?

Answer should include something like the following: Nonviolence could be used as a weapon by a child, a woman, or even a decrepit old man to resist the mightiest government successfully. Although it may seem slow, nonviolence is the surest way to achieve a common goal—and may even "oversweep the world."

Learning Coach Guide
Lesson 2: Linking the Seas and Reaching for the Skies

Lesson Objectives
- Explain the reasons for building a canal across the Isthmus of Panama.
- Identify Lesseps as the builder of the Suez Canal who attempted to build the Panama Canal.
- Recognize the purpose and practice of selling stocks.
- Identify key individuals in the building of the Panama Canal and their accomplishments.
- Summarize the development of the airplane.
- Identify key individuals in the development of air travel.

PREPARE

Approximate lesson time is 60 minutes.

Materials
For the Student
- 🖳 Questions and Answers
- 🖳 Reading Guide

    The Human Odyssey, Volume 2 edited by Klee, Cribb, and Holdren
    History Journal

For the Adult
- 🖳 Lesson Answer Key

Keywords and Pronunciation
Chagres (CHAH-grais)
Gatún (gah-TOON)
George Goethals (GOH-thuhlz)
Louis Blériot (BLER-ee-oh)
Otto Lilienthal (LIL-yuhn-tahl)
Paul Gauguin (goh-GAN)

TEACH
Activity 1: Linking the Seas and Reaching for the Skies (Offline)
Instructions
Day 1
Read

Your student will read Chapter 9, from the beginning to "Reaching for the Sky," pages 655–663, and complete the first part of **Day 1** of the Reading Guide. When he has finished, he should use the Lesson Answer Key to check his work on Day 1, and then place the Reading Guide in his History Journal.

Map Your Way Across Panama

Your student will find out more about the great canal that connected the Atlantic and Pacific Oceans by completing the Panama Map activity. When he has finished, he should compare his answers with the ones in the Lesson Answer Key.

Day 2
Solving the Panama Puzzle

Your student will begin today's lesson online. He will visit the Panama Puzzle website and learn how U.S. Army doctors figured out what caused yellow fever.

Read

Your student will read Chapter 9, from "Reaching for the Sky" to the end, pages 663–667, and complete **Day 2** of the Reading Guide. When he has finished, he should use the Lesson Answer Key to check his work, and then place the Reading Guide in his History Journal.

The Wright Stuff

Your student will go online to "visit" Kitty Hawk and learn more about the achievements of the Wright brothers.

Day 3
Time for a Little Q&A

Your student will get a chance to ask questions of one of the individuals in the chapter by beginning the Q&A activity.

Next, your student will start the answers part of the Q&A activity.

Finally, your student will try to answer the toughest of the questions in the Q&A activity—and come up with a plan for how he can get the answers.

ASSESS
Lesson Assessment: Linking the Seas and Reaching for the Skies, Part 1
(*Online*)

Students will complete an online assessment based on the lesson objectives. The assessment will be scored by the computer. The attached answer key is the most current and may not coincide with previously printed guides.

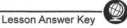

Linking the Seas and Reaching for the Skies

Day 1

Read

Reading Guide

1. For hundreds of years, Europeans had dreamed of a canal across the narrowest part of Central America to connect the <u>Atlantic</u> and the <u>Pacific</u> Oceans. This would eliminate the need to sail all the way around Cape Horn at the southern tip of <u>South America</u>.

2. Finally, they chose a location—the Isthmus of <u>Panama</u>.

3. The man tasked with building the canal was named <u>Ferdinand de Lesseps</u>. He had a good track record, having already built the <u>Suez</u> Canal.

4. What country was he from?
   France

5. To fund the project, he tried to raise money from investors by selling <u>stocks</u>, which are also known as <u>shares</u>. This gave the investors part <u>ownership</u> of the canal company.

6. In the early nineteenth century, which country became involved in the building of the canal?
   the United States

7. Ownership of the canal company shifted. <u>President Theodore Roosevelt</u> arranged to have the United States purchase the French canal company and made the canal's completion a top U.S. priority. <u>John Stevens</u> was the chief engineer who realized that the canal required a series of locks between the two oceans.

8. Name the army doctor who brought yellow fever under control in the canal zone. Who was the military engineer who completed the canal's construction?
   William Crawford Gorgas, George Goethals

Map Your Way Across Panama

1. Assuming it would take approximately 6,000 miles to sail from New York to San Francisco via the Panama Canal, and approximately 14,000 miles via the Cape Horn, how many approximate miles would a ship save by passing through the Panama Canal?
   about 8,000 miles

2. By passing from the Atlantic to the Pacific through the Panama Canal, in which direction is the ship sailing?
   from east to west

3. What landform is the narrow stretch of land that is Panama?
   an isthmus

4. Which South American country used to own this land?
   Colombia

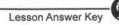

5. We've said that the Panama Canal connects the Atlantic and Pacific Oceans. Which (smaller) bodies of water do they really connect?
    the Caribbean Sea and the Gulf of Panama

6. The Panama Canal isn't the shortest way to connect the two bodies of water. Why did it not follow the shortest route?
    because it had to follow the natural features of the land; because of the jungle and the mountains, the engineers had to pick the easiest (but not necessarily the shortest) route

7. Judging by the scale bar, what is the approximate length of the canal?
    about 50 miles

Day 2

Read

Reading Guide

9. Early aviators such as the German-born <u>Otto Lilienthal</u> flew heavier-than-air aircraft with no engines, known as <u>gliders</u>.

10. <u>The Wright Brothers</u> built a man-sized, engine-powered flying machine that they flew from the sand dunes of North Carolina's Outer Banks.

11. Frenchman Louis Blériot was the first aviator to fly across which body of water?
    the English Channel

12. Eventually, people began to think of practical purposes for flight. Name one of those early uses.
    military purposes, war planes, use in warfare; commercial airlines, planes used to transport people; air circuses in which stunt pilots performed aerial tricks to entertain crowds

Explore and Discuss
This lesson is called Linking the Seas and Reaching for the Skies. These were great transportation achievements in the early twentieth century. What are some of the greatest achievements in the twenty-*first* century? Can you imagine what they might be in the twenty-*second* century?

    Answers may include global satellites that broadcast television images instantaneously around the world; space shuttles that can fly out of the Earth's atmosphere, go into orbit, and land back on an airfield, just like an airplane; "smart" cars with GPS navigation systems that "can be told" where to go; planes that can travel faster than the speed of sound; Concorde planes (now retired) that were so fast that passengers could take off in London and (because of the time difference) land in New York earlier than when they took off; catamaran-style ferries and hovercraft that skim across the surface of the seas.

Learning Coach Guide
Lesson 3. Optional: Your Choice

PREPARE

Approximate lesson time is 60 minutes.

Learning Coach Guide
Lesson 4: Wrapping Up

Lesson Objectives

- Complete a project summarizing historical themes.

PREPARE

Approximate lesson time is 60 minutes.

Materials

For the Student

    🖥 Reading Guide

    🖥 The World Turned Upside Down

    The Human Odyssey, Volume 2 edited by Klee, Cribb, and Holdren

    History Journal

For the Adult

    🖥 Lesson Answer Key

TEACH
Activity 1: Wrapping Up (Online)

Instructions

This lesson is designed to be completed in **2** class sessions.

Day 1

Read

Your student will read the Part 4 Conclusion, from page 668 to page 675, and complete the Reading Guide. When he has finished, he should use the Lesson Answer Key to check his work, and then place the Reading Guide in his History Journal.

A Look Back

Your student will review some of the things he has learned in this unit by completing the Show You Know activity.

The World Turned Upside Down

Your student will chronicle some of the innovations and events that took place in the nineteenth and early twentieth centuries by completing the World Turned Upside Down activity sheet.

Day 2

Dear Granddaughter...

Your student will "look forward" from the early 1900s to preview some of the changes that will take place later in the century in the Dear Granddaughter activity.

ASSESS

Lesson Assessment: Wrapping Up (*Online*)

Use the answer key to evaluate your students' letter and input the total point value in the assessment. The attached answer key is the most current and may not coincide with previously printed guides.

Wrapping Up

Day 1

Read

Reading Guide

1. Sun Yat-sen helped set up the first republic in <u>China</u>, while Mohandas Gandhi was marching in South Africa for the rights of <u>Indians</u>.

2. Name the supposedly unsinkable ship that plunged beneath the waters of the Atlantic on April 14, 1912.
   Titanic

3. Mazzini and Garibaldi helped unite <u>Italy</u>, and Otto von Bismarck forged <u>Germany</u> into a single nation.

4. What were the two main consequences of the American Civil War?
   the end of slavery; the country remained a single nation

5. Name the canal in Egypt that provided European powers with a shortcut to Asia. Name the canal that linked the Atlantic and Pacific Oceans.
   the Suez Canal; the Panama Canal

6. Which "-ism" is concerned with the building of empires?
   imperialism

7. It was said that "the sun never set on the <u>British</u> Empire."

8. Which "-ism" teaches the superiority of one group of people over another?
   racism

9. Which Western ideas helped inspire revolts by subject peoples against world empires?
   nationalism, natural rights, self-rule

10. Name two great empires whose European subjects began to struggle for their freedom.
    the Habsburg or Austro-Hungarian Empire; the Ottoman Empire

11. By the early twentieth century, <u>electricity</u> powered many factories and helped light up homes and streets.

12. Name two ways in which communications improved links between nations.
    The telephone, the telegraph, radio

13. What new high-rise buildings began to appear in cities? Name one new method of transportation in cities. Which New York City suspension bridge was made of twisted steel cables?
    skyscrapers; electric trolleys and underground trains; the Brooklyn Bridge

14. <u>Henry Ford</u> invented the assembly line, which produced automobiles cheaply and efficiently.

15. By 1914, companies in America and Europe were developing what new form of travel?
    air travel

16. That same year, the outbreak of <u>World War I</u> plunged Europe into a conflict that would involve much of the world.

Explore and Discuss

Wow! There were a *lot* of changes during this time period. Most people would say that some of those changes were very good, but that some had both good and bad consequences. Some changes had only negative results. Give an example of each kind of change and evidence to support your answers.

    Answers will vary, but your student should consider both intended and unintended consequences. For example, the automobile improved transportation, provided new jobs in auto-manufacturing and related fields, and made travel possible for many more people than any earlier invention. But the automobile was a major cause of air pollution and traffic deaths.

Lesson Assessment Answer Key

Wrapping Up

Use the answer key to evaluate your students' letter and input the total point value in the assessment.

1. Review your student's letter

   Did your student include:

   - ways in which life might improve in the future (10 points)

   - good things from the previous century that might be lost as the times change (10 points)

   - "How her granddaughter should view change, what she should resist, what she should embrace, and so on." (10 points)

   Total Points: _____
   Enter this number online.

Learning Coach Guide
Lesson 1: End-of-Course Review

Lesson Objectives

- Review knowledge gained in previous lessons and units.
- Demonstrate mastery of important knowledge and skills taught in the Age of Democratic Revolutions unit.
- Demonstrate mastery of important knowledge and skills taught in the Revolutions in Arts, Industries, and Work unit.
- Demonstrate mastery of important knowledge and skills taught in the Nations Unite and Expand unit.
- Demonstrate mastery of important knowledge and skills taught in the Answers and Questions unit.
- Demonstrate mastery of important knowledge and skills taught in The Dawn of the Twentieth Century unit.

PREPARE

Approximate lesson time is 60 minutes.

Materials

For the Student

    🖳 Crossword Puzzle

For the Adult

    🖳 Crossword Puzzle Answer Key

TEACH
Activity 1: Democratic Revolutions, Revolutions in Arts, Industries, and Work

(Online)

Instructions

This lesson is designed to be completed in **3** class sessions.

Day 1

Your student will begin reviewing the Age of Democratic Revolutions and Revolutions in Arts, Industries, and Work units by looking through the following materials in her History Journal.

Completed activity sheets, including Reading Guides

Printouts of online activities

Map activities

Keywords and definitions

Offline assessments

Then your student will go online to complete the following activities:

Declaring Independence

Political Spectrum

Mapping the Growth of an Empire

Urban Problems and Solutions

Flash Cards: Rulers and Revolutionaries

Flash Cards: The Romantics

Unit 11 Review

The History of Flight

Day 2

After reviewing the materials in her History Journal for the Nations Unite and Expand and Answers and Questions units, your student will print out and complete the Cultural World crossword puzzle, and then go online to complete the following activities.

Compare and Contrast: A Unified Italy and Germany

Civil War

Innovators

Spark of Genius

Uniting and Expanding

New York, New York

Triangle Shirtwaist Factory

Women on the March

Turn of the Century

Innovations in Art

Modernistic Trends

Groundbreakers

Day 3

After reviewing the materials in her History Journal for The Dawn of the Twentieth Century unit, your student will read the Epilogue, pages 679–681.

Then your student will go online to complete the following activities.

Heading Toward 1914

Looking Backward, Looking Forward

Activity 2: Looking Backward, Looking Forward (Online)

Name _____   Date _____

Cultural World: Art, Literature, and Music Answer Key

Across:
2. BRAQUE
4. CUBISM
7. CONRAD
9. WORDSWORTH
14. IMPRESSIONISM
16. ABSTRACT
17. ZOLA
18. STOWE
19. BYRON

Down:
1. VANGOGH
3. PICASSO
5. KANDINSKY
6. GOETHE
8. ROMANTICISM
10. FRIEDRICH
11. KIPLING
12. CASSATT
13. DELACROIX
15. STRAVINSKY

Learning Coach Guide
Lesson 2: End-of-Course Assessment

Lesson Objectives

- Demonstrate mastery of the skills and concepts taught in this semester.
- Demonstrate mastery of important knowledge and skills taught in previous lessons.
- Explain why Parliament imposed taxes after 1763 and why the colonists reacted as they did.
- Identify George Washington and his contributions to the revolution.
- Identify the U.S. Constitution as the world's oldest functioning written constitution.
- Summarize Enlightenment ideas that promoted revolution in France.
- Describe the events of the Reign of Terror.
- Explain how Napoleon came to power.
- Identify major positions of the political spectrum.
- Identify significant leaders of nineteenth century Latin American independence movements and their accomplishments and failings.
- Explain why attempts to establish republics in Latin America were less successful than in the United States.
- Describe how Russia differed from western Europe in the sixteenth and seventeenth centuries and explain why.
- Identify Peter the Great.
- Identify Catherine the Great.
- Identify Alexander I.
- Identify major writers, artists, and composers of the Romantic period and the kinds of works they are known for.
- Identify the factors that allowed the Industrial Revolution to begin first in England.
- Identify Adam Smith and what he is known for.
- Describe the advances made in the textile industry in England in the eighteenth century.
- Explain the significance of the steam engine to industry.
- Describe the need for better roads in the 1700s and 1800s and the attempts to improve roads.
- Identify Fulton and his contribution to steam-powered boats.
- Identify Stephenson and his contribution to railroad travel.
- Identify Morse and his contribution to rapid communication.
- Describe conditions for factory workers in the early nineteenth century.
- Describe living conditions for poor workers in industrial cities.
- Identify Charles Dickens and the impact of his writing.
- Identify Karl Marx and what he is known for.
- Identify Charles Darwin and what he is known for.
- Describe the slave trade in Africa as it existed by 1700.
- Describe the transatlantic slave trade and its consequences.
- Identify the causes of Italian and German unification.
- Identify Jefferson Davis and Abraham Lincoln and what they are known for.

- Summarize the results of the American Civil War.
- Identify Alexander Graham Bell and his accomplishments.
- Identify Thomas Edison and his accomplishments.
- Identify Guglielmo Marconi and his accomplishments.
- Describe advances in fuels in the late 1800s.
- Explain how steel led to a second industrial revolution.
- Explain the reasons for the New Imperialism.
- Identify on a map the major areas of colonization by Britain, Belgium, Japan, France, Russia, and the United States.
- Explain the reasons for the population growth in cities of the 1800s.
- Identify Louis Pasteur and describe his accomplishments.
- Summarize the methods Henry Ford used to bring automobiles to the masses.
- Identify examples of Impressionist, Postimpressionist, Cubist, and abstract art and artists.
- Identify Sun Yat-sen and his role in Chinese independence.
- Identify key individuals in the building of the Panama Canal and their accomplishments.
- Summarize the development of the airplane.
- Summarize Gandhi's development as a champion of Indian independence from Britain.
- Define *nationalism*.
- Recognize Napoleon's role in the nationalist movements of the nineteenth century in Europe.
- Describe the effects of colonization on the peoples of the colonized territories.
- Describe the conditions city dwellers faced in places such as Paris, London, and New York.
- Recognize the Serbs as an example of ethnic groups whose nationalism led to independence movements within the Ottoman Empire.
- Describe the role of nationalism in changing imperialism in the early twentieth century.

PREPARE

Approximate lesson time is 60 minutes.

ASSESS

Semester Assessment: End-of-Course Assessment, Part 1 (*Online*)

Students will complete an online assessment based on the course objectives. The assessment will be scored by the computer. The attached answer key is the most current and may not coincide with previously printed guides.

Semester Assessment: End-of-Course Assessment, Part 2 (*Offline*)

Students will complete this part of the Course Assessment offline. Print the test and have students complete it on their own. Use the answer key to score the test, and then enter the results online. The attached answer key is the most current and may not coincide with previously printed guides.
